TRADE AND DEVELOPMENT IN TRANSITIONAL ECONOMIES

TRADE AND DEVELOPMENT IN TRANSITIONAL ECONOMIES

KISHOR SHARMA

Nova Science Publishers, Inc.
New York

For permission to use material from this book please contact us:
Telephone 631-231-7269; Fax 631-231-8175
Web Site: http://www.novapublishers.com

Library of Congress Cataloging-in-Publication Data

Sharma, Kishor.
Trade and development in transitional economies / Kishor Sharma.
p. cm.
Includes index.
ISBN 1-59454-816-1
1. Kyrgyzstan--Commercial policy. 2. Tajikistan--Commercial policy. 3. Kyrgyzstan--Economic policy--1991- 4. Tajikistan--Economic policy--1991- I. Title.
HF1586.44.S43 2006
338.95843--dc22 2005029731

Published by Nova Science Publishers, Inc. ✢New York

CONTENTS

Preface		**vii**
Chapter 1	Purpose, Scope and Profile of Central Asia	**1**
Chapter 2	Trade and Development: Theory and Empirical Evidence	**23**
Chapter 3	Policy Development in Kyrgyz Republic and Tajikistan	**45**
Chapter 4	Trade in Transitional Economies: Kyrgyz Republic and Tajikistan	**65**
Chapter 5	Development Challenges of Kyrgyz Republic and Tajikistan	**85**
Chapter 6	Policy Options for Kyrgyz Republic and Tajikistan	**95**
Appendix I	Socio-Economic Indicators of Kyrgyzstan	**103**
Appendix II	Socio-Economic Indicators of Tajikistan	**109**
Appendix III	The General Agreement on Tariff and Trade (GATT 1947)	**115**
Appendix IV	Business Climate in the Caucasus, Central Asia, Russia, Ukraine, Belarus and Moldova Obstacles to Doing Business; Caucasus, Central Asian, and the Slavic Republics' Ratings among 22 World Regions	**117**
Appendix V	Export Value Growth and Share in Total Exports of the 20 Most Market-Dynamic Products, 1980-1998 (Per Cent)	**119**

Appendix VI Engagement of CIS-5 Countries in International and Regional Arrangements **121**

Appendix VII The Main International Road and Rail Transport Agreements and Conventions Ratified by CIS-5, as of February 15, 2002 **123**

Appendix VIII Integration with the Global Economy: Central Asian Countries in the Global Context **125**

Bibliography **127**

Index **135**

PREFACE

As a teacher of International Trade and Development, I always find it frustrating when graduate students complain about the lack of resources on trade and development issues, especially on newly independent states that have emerged after the collapse of the former Soviet Union (FSU). Not only are analytical books limited but also there is a lack of data on these countries to carry out any systematic analysis. This motivated me to write a comprehensive book on trade and development challenges of such countries, based on both primary and secondary data. Due to time and resource constraints, however, I limited my analysis to Kyrgyz Republic and Tajikistan whose experiences are equally important to other newly independent countries. These countries were little known to the rest of the world until they gained independence from the FSU. Independence from the FSU brought more challenges than opportunities. Despite huge development potential, based on natural resources, almost all countries in the region continue to suffer from high unemployment and fiscal imbalances. While trade, based on the concept of comparative advantage, is crucial for small economies, as the experience of Singapore and Hong Kong suggests, it has not played a significant role in accelerating growth and alleviating poverty in the Central Asian countries. This book sheds light on these issues which can provide useful development lessons, not only to newly independent countries, but also to other developing countries which are in the path of global integration.

Some of the data presented in this book were collected during my visit to the region in 2003 which was funded by the Asian Development Bank. I am grateful to the Bank for granting me this opportunity. Last, but not least, I thank my wife Sushma Sharma and children Shristy, Dristy and Prashant for supporting me while I was working on this manuscript. I also thank Ms. Kerry Cutting for help with word processing and formatting.

Kishor Sharma
Charles Sturt University
Wagga Wagga, NSW, Australia
15 February 2005

Chapter 1

PURPOSE, SCOPE AND PROFILE OF CENTRAL ASIA

INTRODUCTION

The second half of the 20th Century witnessed major developments in international politics and economics. The creation of international institutions (such as the UN system, World Bank and more recently WTO (World Trade Organization)), the fall of the Berlin wall and collapse of former Soviet Union (FSU), and widespread removal of barriers to trade and investment by the majority of countries are diverse examples. These developments have promoted greater integration of the global economy, reflected in increased mobility of goods, people and capital between countries. Together with developments in transport and especially communications, this has significantly increased economic interdependence among countries, leading to an unprecedented growth in world output and international trade. For example, during 1947-97, world output grew six-fold whilst international trade increased 16-fold (Sharma and Morrissey, 2005). As output and trade increased, millions of people were lifted out of poverty in many developing countries, particularly in those that embarked on outward looking strategies while countries that continued with inward looking strategies lagged behind. The latter group of countries continued to perform poorly in terms of output, exports and employment growth which led to severe macro-economic imbalances. By the early 1990s, mounting fiscal crises, on one hand, and the growing pressure from international institutions, on the other, forced these countries to embark on outward looking strategies. Countries that fall in this group included not only African, and South and East Asian countries but also countries from Central Asia and Eastern Europe which were the part of the FSU. With the collapse of FSU the Central Asian countries (namely Kazakhstan, Kyrgyz Republic, Tajikistan, Turkmenistan and Uzbekistan) - which were little known to the rest of the world - emerged as independent states in the early 1990s after being part of the former Soviet Union for about 70 years. All of these countries are small in terms of national income and population. Population range from less than 5 million in Kyrgyz Republic to about 15 million in Kazakhstan, while the per capita income varies from US$1,200 in Kazakhstan to US$160 in Tajikistan. All Central Asian countries are land-locked and they all have to cross at least two or three country's territories in order to reach international market outside their region. A map presented on the next page shows the location of the Central Asian Republics. The location of Kyrgyz Republic and Tajikistan are shaded in the map.

At the time of independence, it was thought that international integration would help these countries through a number of channels. Firstly, international integration allows resource allocation in line with a nation's comparative advantage, which in turn enhances export potential. Export growth is an indirect way of increasing income and consumption and improving living standards. Secondly, foreign exchange earned through exports permits firms to import superior technologies and inputs, which improve efficiency in both exportable as well as import-substitution industries. Thirdly, international integration, by enhancing export opportunities, allows firms to enjoy the benefits of large-scale production. Fourthly, increased exposure brought about by exporting and importing opportunities encourages firms to adopt best practices and maintain quality, leading to an improvement in efficiency. Fifthly, removal of distortion and greater international integration attract foreign investment in the areas of a nation's comparative advantage, which helps create jobs and alleviates poverty. Foreign investment is essential for developing countries which lack financial resources, managerial know-how, technology and marketing networks

Despite these obvious benefits of global integration, countries in Central Asia have not benefited much from an outward-oriented strategy. In fact, disintegration from the FSU brought more challenges than opportunities.

Although the East Asian experience suggests that economic growth and poverty alleviation appear to be linked with an outward-oriented strategy, their experience is less relevant to countries in Central Asia which lack efficient institutions and infrastructures. In fact, efficient institutions, infrastructure and open political systems are the basic prerequisites for globalization to succeed.

Figure 1.1. Map of Central Asia Republics

Those states that failed to develop good governance, efficient institutions and infrastructure are likely to find themselves falling further behind in development efforts (Gleason, 2003). In other words, globalization rewards those countries that can develop these as they embark on international integration and punishes those countries that failed to develop these. While Central Asia countries have gone a long way in opening up their economies through reform in their trade, investment and payment policies, very little progress has been made in developing good governance and creating efficient institutions and infrastructure. The access to international market remains a major problem due to the lack of efficient transport network and time consuming customs and border formalities. The enforcement of law and order is very weak and protection of private property remains a major problem. Also, very little progress has been made towards democracy which is crucial for developing private sector confidence. While all Central Asia countries are ruled by elected Presidents none of the country's elections appeared to have been conducted in a fair manner. These Presidents exercise their power to rule the country by decree with the force of 'constitutional law' (Gleason, 2003). In this situation, violation of human rights and corruption are common in all countries.

It is in this context that this book aims to identify development challenges that Kyrgyz Republic and Tajikistan face in their attempt towards global integration. The purpose of choosing these two countries is guided by the fact that Kyrgyz Republic is already a member of the WTO, while Tajikistan is in the advance stage of gaining its membership. Both countries have similar resource endowment and they have similar per capita income. A comparative study of these two countries would provide useful lessens not only for countries in Central Asian but also to other developing countries which are in the path of global integration.

PROFILE OF CENTRAL ASIA

The Central Asian countries consist of Kazakhstan, Kyrgyz Republic[1], Tajikistan, Turkmenistan and Uzbekistan. These countries are surrounded by China in the east, the Caspian Sea in the west, Central Siberia in the north, and Afghanistan and Iran in the south. Five Central Asian countries together cover about 3,995 thousand square kms and provide shelter for about 52 million people (less than 1% of the world population). By developing countries standards, their social indicators are high. As shown in Table 1.1, access to medical facilities and

[1] Kyrgyz Republic is also known as Kyrgyzstan.

sanitation in these countries is as high as middle income countries, thanks to the legacy of the Soviet Union.

The average per capita income of the region is about US$611, although it varies considerably between the countries. For example, Kazakhstan has the highest per capita income (US$1,230) while Tajikistan has the lowest (US$157) (Pomfret, 2005). Kyrgyzstan and Tajikistan are the poorest countries in the region with per capita income of US$279 and US$157 respectively. The region has abundant supplies of gas, oil, mineral and water resources, although they are not yet fully utilized. Except for Kazakhstan, which is rich in petroleum products, agriculture is an important sector for most countries in terms of its contribution to Gross Domestic Product (GDP) and employment creation. The share of agriculture in GDP varies from 54% in Kyrgyz Republic to 10% in Kazakhstan and 29% in Tajikistan (Table 1.2). Although each country has its own language, they share common cultures and have a common religion (Moslem). All five countries are land-locked economies.

Despite these common features, there are diversities between the countries. For example, like other countries, Kyrgyz Republic and Tajikistan do not have significant gas and oil deposits, but they have abundant supplies of water resources, making them major producers and suppliers of hydro-electricity in the region. Both Kyrgyz Republic and Tajikistan also have some mineral reserves. The former is endowed with gold reserves[2] while the latter has an abundant reserve of aluminium. However, these resources are not yet fully exploited. The industrial sector is more diversified in Kazakhstan and Turkmenistan than any other countries in the region and most of their GDP is derived from industrial and service sectors.

Following independence all Central Asian countries experienced macroeconomic crisis mainly due to the loss of subsidies from the FSU and a fall in output. Output declined partly due to the loss of Soviet markets and partly due to the lack of institutions and infrastructure. Even by 1998, they had not achieved the pre-independence output level. The ratio of post to pre-transition output level indicates that by 1998, the Central Asian countries as a group, had achieved less than 60% of the pre-transition output level. However, there are significant variations between the countries, for example Uzbekistan reached 90% of the pre-transition output level while Tajikistan achieved only 42% (Table 1.2). Table 1.2 presents selected indicators of the Central Asian countries.

[2]Kyrgyz Republic's Kumtor gold mine is the eighth largest in the world.

Table 1.1. Service Indicators for Central Asian Countries and Major Regions

	Primary pupil-teacher ratio	Trained teachers in primary education	Child immunization rate		Physicians	Hospital beds	Inpatient admission rate	Access to an improved water source	Access to improved sanitation facilities
	Pupils per teacher	% of total	% of children under age one		Per 1,000 people	Per 1,000 people	% of population	% of population	% of population
	2000	2000	Measles 2001	DPT 2001	1995-2000 [a]	1995-2000[a]	1995-2000[a]	2000	2000
Kazakhstan	19	-	96	96	3.5	8.5	15	91	99
Kyrgyz Rep	24	48.5	99	99	3.0	9.5	21	77	100
Tajikistan	22	-	86	83	2.0	-	-	60	90
Turkmenistan	-	-	98	95	3.0	-	-	-	-
Uzbekistan	-	-	99	97	3.1	8.3	-	85	89
World	27 m	- m	72 w	73 w	- w	- w	9 w	81 w	55 w
Low income	*39*	78.9	59	61	-	-		76	43
Middle income	*21*	-	86	85	1.9	3.3	6	82	60
Lower middle income	*21*	-	85	84	1.9	3.3	6	81	58
Upper middle income	21	-	91	92	1.8	3.3	11	-	-
Low and middle income	*29*	-	71	71	-	-		79	51
East Asia and Pacific	*21*	-	76	77	1.7	2.4	4	76	46
Europe and Central Asia	-	-	95	94	3.1	8.9	18	91	-
Latin America and Carib	26	-	91	89	1.5	2.2	2	86	77
Middle East and N Africa	24	-	92	92	-	-		88	85
South Asia	*42*	66.5	58	65	-	-		84	34
Sub-Saharan Africa	47	78.9	58	53	-	-		58	53
High income	17	-	90	94	3.0	7.4	15	-	

Note: For data comparability and overage, see the technical notes. Figures in italics are for years other than those specified.
a. Data are for the most recent year available. b. Average for 14 states. m refers to median values. w refers to weighted average.
Source: World Bank (2004), *World Development Report 2004 Making services for poor people*

Table 1.2. Selected Indicators of Central Asian Countries

	Population (million)			GDP Per capita (US$)			% Contribution to GDP of #			Ratio of Real GDP 1998/1989	Trade % of GDP	
	1990	1995	2000	1990	1995	2000	Agricul-ture	Industry	Others	1998/89	1995	2000
Kazakhstan	16.35	15.80	14.87	4,810	1,053	1,230	10	33	56	0.61	78	78
Kyrgyz Republic	4.34	4.62	4.94	195*	323	279	54	17	29	0.60	67	83
Tajikistan	5.30	5.84	6.29	-	84	157	29	26	45	0.42	344	161
Turkmenistan	3.76	4.53	5.28	1,515*	1,302	833	26	38	36	0.44	55	95
Uzbekistan	20.52	22.79	20.60	2,724	446	559	34	16	50	0.90	75	52

* Data for 1993. # Based on 2000 GDP.

Notes: Industry sector includes mining, manufacturing, electricity, gas and water. Others include construction, trade, transport and communication, and finance.

Sources: ADB (2002a), 'Key Indicators of Developing Asian and Pacific Countries 2002', except for the ratio of real GDP: 1998/89 which is taken from Siegelbaum et. al. (2002).

Until 1990, institutions, infrastructure and welfare system of all five Central Asian countries were managed by the FSU. Government had complete control over trade and commerce as well as agricultural land, minerals and other natural resources. Achieving self-sufficiency was one of the major aims during the Soviet regime. This led to the development of industries to cater for the regional markets and serve the regional interests, without paying enough attention to costs. Transport networks, namely road and railways, were developed to support these objectives, again without paying any attention to efficiency. Since there were no barriers to trade between the members of the FSU and infrastructure network was designed to promote trade among themselves, intra-regional trade was a significant part of total trade. By late 1980s, the share of intra-regional trade in total trade was over 85% (Pomfret 1995).

Barter trade was the popular means of exchange and bureaucrats had the control over trade and investment decisions. Exports were regulated mainly to ensure enough supplies of food and other essential items for domestic consumption. All economic and social activities were managed by the state and the basic services, such as natural gas, electricity, water supply and transportation, were subsidized to achieve the social welfare objective. Under these circumstances there was little incentive to set up activities in which they had a natural comparative advantage, particularly labour-intensive, leading to a high rate of unemployment. However, the severity of unemployment was not visible due to the legacy of the welfare system supported by the Soviet Union. With the disintegration from the FSU, the Central Asian countries experienced a dramatic decline in output, a rise in current account deficit and hyper-inflation. Although deteriorating macro-economic conditions have been arrested, these economies remain fragile mainly due to the lack of efficient institutions, infrastructure and good governance.

In the immediate transition period, all five countries experienced a fall in output, hyper-inflation and a rise in current account deficit (Table 1.3). Countries that have made good progress in GDP growth are Turkmenistan and Uzbekistan. Although Kyrgyz Republic and Tajikistan have arrested a declining trend in GDP since mid 1990s, their growth performance has been much lower than the other countries in the region (Table 1.3). In terms of GDP growth, Kyrgyz Republic is the poor performer.

Table 1.3. Key Macroeconomic Indicators of Central Asian Countries

	1990	1992	1994	1996	1998	2000	2001	2002	2003	2004
Growth in Real GDP										
Kazakhstan	-0.4	-2.9	-12.6	0.5	-2.5	9.8	13.2	9.8	9.2	9.3
Kyrgyz	0.3	-19.0	-20.0	7.1	1.8	5.4	5.3	0.0	6.7	5.3
Tajikistan	-1.6	-29.0	-18.9	-4.4	5.3	8.3	10.0	9.5	10.2	6.0
Turkmenistan	2.0	-5.3	-18.8	-8.0	4.2	17.6	20.5	21.2	23.1	10.5
Uzbekistan	1.6	-11.1	-4.2	1.6	3.3	49.6	53.8	4.2	4.4	2.8
Inflation (Change in CPI in %)										
Kazakhstan	104.6	2,984.1	1,160.0	28.6	8.3	13.2	8.4	5.9	6.4	6.7
Kyrgyz	170.0*	1,259.0	95.7	35.0	10.4	18.7	6.9	2.1	3.1	4.0
Tajikistan	204.0*	1,364.0	1.1	40.1	-	32.9	38.5	10.2	17.1	15.0
Turkmenistan	155.0*	644.0	1,328.0	446.0	-	7.4	6.0	10.6	6.5	9.0
Uzbekistan	169.0	910.0	885.0	64.0	9.5`	3.2	2.0	24.2	13.1	8.3
Central Government Balance (% of GDP)										
Kazakhstan	1.4	-7.3	-7.5	-4.2	-3.9	-0.1	-0.6	-.03	-0.9	-1.9
Kyrgyz	0.3	-17.4	-11.6	-9.5	-4.6	-10.0	-4.0	-5.4	-5.0	-4.4
Tajikistan	-16.4*	-30.5	-5.4	-5.8	-2.9	-0.4	-0.2	-0.1	0.9	-0.5
Turkmenistan	1.2	13.2	-1.4	-0.2	-2.6	-0.3	-0.9	-	-	-
Uzbekistan	-1.1	-18.4	-6.1	-7.3	-	-	-	-	-	-
Current Account Balance (% of GDP)										
Kazakhstan	-	-31.5	-7.7	-3.6	-5.6	-4.1	-4.6	-3.5	-0.2	-0.2
Kyrgyz	-	-1.8	-11.3	-23.6	-16.7	-5.6	-0.7	-1.2	-2.2	-1.7
Tajikistan	-	18.4	-21.0	-7.3	-10.8	-5.9	-7.7	-2.7	-1.3	-2.2
Turkmenistan	-	14.1	3.8	2.2	-45.8	-13.0	-	-4.9	6.0	8.0
Uzbekistan	-	-11.9	2.1	-8.6	-1.7	-	-	-1.0	2.3	7.5

Note: * 1991

Sources: EBRD (1999); ADB (2002a, 2002b and 2004)

Table 1.4. Foreign aid Recipient Indicators for Central Asian Countries and Major Regions

	Net official development assistance or official aid		Aid per capita				Aid dependency ratios					
	$ millions		$		Aid as % of GNI		Aid as % of gross capital formation		Aid as % of imports of goods and services		Aid as % of central government expenditure	
	1996	**2001**	**1996**	**2001**	**1996**	**2001**	**1996**	**2001**	**1996**	**2001**	**1996**	**2001**
Kazakhstan	125	148	8	10	0.6	0.7	3.7	2.6	1.6	1.3	-	4.6
Kyrgyz Rep	231	188	50	38	12.9	12.9	50.19	68.5	21.4	29.2	56.5	69.5
Tajikistan	103	159	17	25	10.5	15.5	44.0	124.0	11.7	18.4	-	129.1
Turkmenistan	24	72	5	13	1.0	1.2	-	3.3	1.2	2.3	-	-
Uzbekistan	88	153	4	6	0.6	1.4	2.2	6.6	1.8	4.5	-	-
World	62,264 s	58,244 s	11 w	10 w	0.2 w	0.2 w	0.9 w	0.9 w	0.8 w	0.6 w	- w	- w
Low income	24,618	24,611	11	10	2.6	2.5	10.4	10.9	9.4	8.4	-	-
Middle income	22,401	21,006	9	8	0.4	0.4	1.7	1.7	1.6	1.3	-	-
Lower middle income	18,557	17,145	8	7	0.5	0.5	1.9	1.9	2.3	1.8	-	-
Upper middle income	3,175	3,336	10	10	0.3	0.2	1.0	0.9	0.6	0.5	-	-
Low and middle income	58,925	57,208	12	11	1.0	0.9	3.9	3.9	3.6	2.9	-	-
East Asia and Pacific	8,039	7,394	5	4	0.6	0.5	1.4	1.3	1.6	1.2	-	-
Europe and Central Asia	8,670	9,783	18	21	0.8	1.0	3.3	4.4	2.4	2.3	-	-
Latin America and Carib	7,430	4,985	15	12	0.4	0.3	1.8	1.6	1.9	1.2	-	-
Middle East and N Africa	5,884	4,836	22	16	1.0	0.7	5.0	3.3	3.6	2.7	-	-
South Asia	5,169	5,871	4	4	1.0	1.0	4.7	4.3	5.5	5.1	-	-
Sub-Saharan Africa	16,552	13,933	28	21	5.2	4.6	27.3	24.6	14.2	11.0	-	-
High income	3,339	1,036	4	1	0.0	0.0	1.2	0.0	0.1	0.0	-	-

Note: Regional aggregates include date for economies not specified elsewhere. World and income group totals include aid not allocated by country or region. The 2001 data exclude aid from the World Food Programme.

s refers to simple sums of data.; w refers to weighted averages

Source: World Bank (2004).

Table 1.5. Income, Consumption and Distribution in Central Asian Countries, 1996-2000

	Per Capita Income			Per Capita Consumption			Share of 1st Quintile			Share of 5th Quintile			Gini			Survey Type
	1960	**1980**	**2000**	**1960**	**1980**	**2000**	**1960**	**1980**	**2000**	**1960**	**1980**	**2000**	**1960**	**1980**	**2000**	
Kazakhstan	-	-	5,521	-	-	3,950	9.5	9.5	6.1	35.2	35.2	43.1	-	-	36.9	Exp.
Kyrgyzstan	-	-	2,822	-	-	2,191	4.3	4.3	10.7	48.7	48.7	34.3	-	-	23.6	Inc.
Tajikistan	2,052	3,493		1,119	1,904	-	-	-	-	-	-	-	-	-	-	
Turkmenistan	4,411	7,508	4,060	2,223	3,784	2,534	10.0	10.0	6.7	36.6	36.6	42.8	26.7	26.7	36.0	Inc.
Uzbekistan	-	-	24,70	-	-	1,841	10.6	10.6	7.4	35.6	35.6	40.9	-	-	33.5	Inc.

Note: Exp. = Based on expenditure data
Inc. = Based on income data
(i) Annual per capita income and consumption data are in purchasing power parity dollars at 2000 prices (1993 base year).
(ii).The shares of 1st and 5th quintile represent the quintile shares on income or consumption depending on the type of survey
Source: Balla (2002)

Since late 1990s, tight monetary and fiscal policies brought inflation under control in all countries, except Tajikistan. High inflation in Tajikistan appears to be mainly due to supply-side rigidities, namely the poor internal transport and the lack of finance for productive activities. All five countries have made progress in controlling budget deficit. By 2001, budget deficits in Kyrgyz Republic and Tajikistan were brought down to 4% and 0.2% of GDP respectively. This has been achieved mainly through privatization of public enterprises and price liberalization. The current account deficit has also been brought under control in all five countries. By 2001, the current account deficit as percentage of GDP was 0.7% in Kyrgyz Republic and 7.7% in Tajikistan.

Following disintegration from the FSU, all Cental Asian countries experienced a loss in institutions, infrastructure and revenue. In this regard, official development assistance has played a crucial role in reversing this trend, although there is a long way to go. During the 1996 to 2001 period, except for Kyrgyz Republic, all countries in the region experienced a significant growth in foreign aid. Although aid flows to Kyrgyz Republic declined during this period, she is still the largest recipient of development assistance in the region. This appears to be mainly due to her commitments to open up its economy. It should be noted that foreign aid is the major source of capital formation in all Cental Asian countries. In Kyrgyz Republic foreign aid contributes about 68% to gross capital formation, while in Tajikistan 124% (Table 1.4).

Although macro-economic stability has been achieved mainly through tight monetary and fiscal policies, very little efforts have been made to diversify the production base. This has not only increased unemployment and poverty but also increased inequality. In all Central Asian countries a small number of population enjoys a significant proportion of national income (Table 1.5).

PROFILE OF KYRGYZ REPUBLIC AND TAJIKISTAN

Kyrgyz Republic

Kyrgyz Republic is surrounded by Kazakhstan in the north, Republic of China in the east, Tajikistan in the south and Uzbekistan in the west. It spreads to 200 thousand square kms and provides shelter for less than 5 million people, making it the smallest country in the region (Table 1.2). Agriculture is the major source of income, which contributes 54% to GDP and employs 49% of the work force. Within agriculture, the livestock is an important sector, although per capita productivity (yield per animal) is very low. Trade, transport, communication and finance together contribute 29% to GDP and employ about 40% of the work force. Manufacturing, mining and energy contribute about 17% to GDP and employ 9% of the work force. Table 1.6 presents key indicators of Kyrgyzstan.

Figure 1.2 below shows structure of output in Kyrgyz Republic during the 1990 to 2003 period. Agriculture is by far the most important sector in Kyrgyzstan and the contribution of the services and industry sectors have significantly varied over the years. The industry sector, which also includes mining, contributes less than one fourth to GDP, while this share of services is over one third in GDP (in 2003). Appendix I presents socio-economic indicators of Kyrgyzstan.

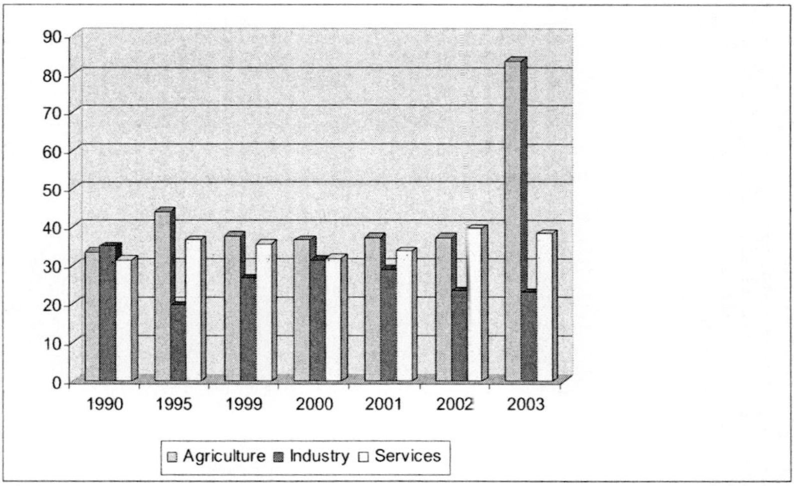

Source: ADB (2004)

Figure 1.2. Structure of Output Percentage of GDP

Table 1.6. Kyrgyzstan Key Indices: Production

Item	1991	1992	1993	1994	1995	1996	1997	1998	1999	2000	2001	2002
Population (million: as of July 1)	4.39	4.49	4.48	4.47	4.62	4.69	4.76	4.83	4.90	4.97	4.95	4.98
GDP at 1990 constant market (mn soms)	39.4	34.0	28.7	22.9	21.7	23.2	25.5	26.0	27.0	28.5	30.0	29.8
prices Labour force (thousand: calendar year)	-	-	1710	1716	1741	1791	1792	1811	1901	1911	1926	-
Employed	1754	1836	1681	1645	1641	1651	1689	1705	1764	1767	1774	1775
Agriculture	623	70	669	686	771	778	816	837	924	938	944	-
Manufacturing	466	414	359	318	271	241	228	219	204	202	182	-
Others	665	722	653	641	599	632	645	649	636	627	648	-
Unemployed	-	-	29	71	100	140	103	106	137	144	152	-
Unemployment rate (%)	-	-	1.7	4.1	5.7	7.8	5.7	5.9	7.2	7.5	7.9	-
Production (thousand metric tons: calendar year												
Agriculture, crop year												
1 Wheat	434	634	831	566	625	964	1274	1204	1109	1039	11,190	-
2 Barley	557	582	477	288	159	166	152	162	180	150	140	-
3 Potatoes	326	362	308	311	432	562	678	774	957	1046	1168	-
4 Maize	365	281	184	129	116	182	171	228	308	338	443	-
5 Vegetables (fresh, frozen, etc.)	399	404	259	266	318	369	479	556	719	747	815	-
6 Meat	230	228	214	197	180	186	186	191	196	196	197	201
7 Milk	1131	961	946	872	864	885	912	973	1064	1105	1142	1173
Production indexes period averages												
Agriculture (1985 / 1989-91 = 100)	107.0	100.6	97.0	88.0	81.2	89.8	97.9	100.8	106.3	107.7	111.2	113.0
Industry (1985 / 1995 = 100)	118.0	87.0	65.0	47.0	100.0	108.8	163.6	178.0	170.5	185.7	194.1	142.0
Energy (annual values)												
Coal ('000 m.t.)												
Production	-	2151	1721	848	463	410	522	432	417	419	475	498
Exports	-	1024	531	171	171	100	78	23	11	22	19	101
Imports	-	1339	1028	1355	500	844	290	806	764	726	343	883
Consumption	-	2465	2218	2032	792	1154	734	1215	1170	1123	801	-
Electricity (mn kWh)												
Production	14,171	11,892	11,091	12,932	12,349	13,758	12,637	11,618	13,119	14,886	13,667	11,902
Exports	-	-	-	-	1622	2881	2417	998	2011	3153	2165	1062
Imports	-	-	-	-	254	815	715	394	184	321	322	385
Consumption	8814	8616	8467	8189	10,981	11,678	10,854	10,893	11,262	12,054	11,797	-

Source: Asian Development Bank (2002c and 2003)

While there is an enormous potential in hydro-electricity generation, currently only about 10% of electricity is generated from the water resources. Kyrgyz Republic is a mountainous country and is known as the "Switzerland of Asia" for its natural beauty (Pomfret, 1995). Tourism has a great potential in the long run. However, this is only possible by developing transport networks, proper marketing and maintaining law and order in the country.

Kyrgyz Republic is one of the poorest countries in the world. About 50% of the people live below the poverty line. In fact, its GDP at 1990s constant prices, has fallen from 39.4 million soms in 1991 to 29.8 million soms by 2002 (Table 1.6). This has significantly increased its reliance on external debt which has been rising from 33% of GDP in 1990 to 110% by 2001. Despite a huge requirement for developmental investment, gross fixed capital formation has been declining. Appendix I presents socio-economic indicators of Kyrgyzstan. During the 1990 to 2003 period, gross fixed capital formation as percentage of GDP fell from 24% to 16% (Table 1.7). This appears to be mainly due to a poor business climate caused by the lack of effective enforcement of law and order in the country, weak institutions and infrastructure, and time consuming customs and cross-border formalities (see Chapter 4 for further discussion on this). Table 1.7 presents key economic indicators of Kyrgyzstan.

Table 1.7. Key Economic Indicators of Kyrgyzstan

	Kyrgyz Republic			
	1990	**2001**	**2002**	**2003**
Gross Fixed Capital Formation % of GDP	24.29	18.0	17.6	16.2
Exports of Goods and Services % of GDP	29.20	36.54	43.31	41.8
Per Capita FDI (US$)	3.03	4.43	1.01	3.40
External Debt % of GD1	41.00[b]	142.10	117.30	116.40
Debt Service % of Export of goods and services	13.20[b]	27.40[c]	29.80	25.30
Gross Domestic Saving % of GDP	4.20[a]	12.60	13.60	11.6

a = 1995, b 1993 c 1994

Source: ADB (2002a and 2005), and EBRD (1999)

Although Kyrgyz Republic has a fully functional parliament, which consists of a Legislative Assembly of 35 deputies and a People's Representative Assembly of 70 deputies, it has poor governance and human right indicators. The governance indicators indicate that corruption is high, law enforcement is weak and political stability remains a problem (Table 1.8).

Table 1.8. World Bank Institute Governance Indicators for Kyrgyzstan

Governance indicator	Year	Percentile rank (0-100) in %	Estimate (-2.5 to +2.5)	Standard deviation	Number of surveys/ polls
Voice and accountability	2000/01	31.6	-0.57	0.19	3
Political stability/No violence	2000/01	39.5	-0.32	0.48	2
Government effectiveness	2000/01	31.9	-0.61	0.31	3
Regulatory quality	2000/01	20.7	-0.63	0.37	4
Rule of law	2000/01	26.5	-0.72	0.22	4
Control of corruption	2000/01	20.5	-0.85	0.23	4

Source: Gleason (2003)

Republic of Tajikistan

The Republic of Tajikistan borders with Afghanistan in the south (1,030 km), People Republic of China in the east (430 km), Kyrgyz Republic in the north (590 km) and Uzbekistan in the west (950 km). It occupies 134 thousand square kilometres (kms). Like Kyrgyz Republic, Tajikistan is a mountainous country and high mountains cover about 93% of the landscape. The mountainous landscape makes it difficult in winter to reach the east or north of the country by road without taking a detour through Uzbekistan and Kyrgyz Republic.

Its economy is highly dependent on foreign trade and trade flows are much higher than GDP. Agriculture is the backbone of the economy, contributing about one quarter to GDP and two third to employment (in 2001). Mining and energy contribute about 21% to GDP, while the share of service sector is about 50%. The service sector has grown rapidly since the late 1990s, thanks to privatization of transportation, communication and commercial activities earlier managed by the government. Figure 1.3 shows structure of output in Tajikistan during 1995 to 2002.

Tajikistan's has suffered significantly due to the civil war that lasted for five years (1992-97) and claimed about 50,000 human lives. Many technocrats and entrepreneurs left the country during the war and the physical infrastructure was badly damaged. Despite huge demand for investment, particularly in the infrastructure sector, gross fixed capital formation has significantly fallen. During the 1990 to 2001 period, it fell by about 50% from 22% of GDP in 1990 to 11.6% in 2001 (Table 1.9).

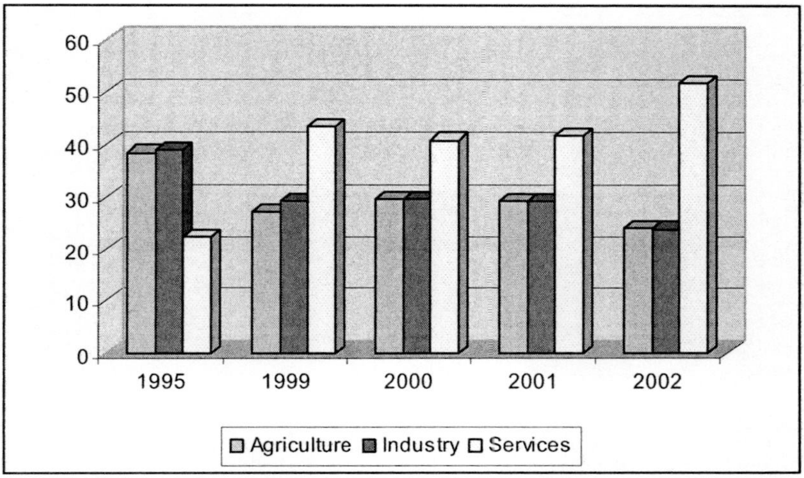

Source: ADB (2004).

Figure 1.3. Structure of Output in Tajikistan (% of GDP at current price)

Table 1.9. Key Economic Indicators of Tajikistan

	Tajikistan		
	1990	**2001**	**2002**
Gross Fixed Capital Formation % of GDP	28.7 [a]	17.00 [b]	227.0
Exports of Goods and Services % of GDP	79.1	61.60 [b]	58.42
Per Capita FDI (US$)	1.54 [c]	1.59	5.6
External Debt % of GDI	102.7 [a]	108.1	99.9
Debt Service as % of export of goods and services	6.8 [a]	11.5	10.3

a 1995; b 2000; c 1993

Source: ADB (2002a and 2004)

Table 1.10. Key Production Indices of Tajikistan

Item	1991	1992	1993	1994	1995	1996	1997	1998	1999	2000	2001	2002
Population (million: as of July 1)	5.46	5.57	5.64	5.75	5.84	5.93	6.02*	6.11*	6.20*	6.29*		
GDP at current market prices	-	-	-	-	69.8	308.5	518.4	1025.2	1344.9	1806.8	6.31	6.44*
Labour force (thousand: calendar		1915	1876	1886	1891	1777	1842	1855	1780*	1794*	2528.8	3345.6
year)	-	1908	1854	1854	1853	1731	1791	1796	1726*	1745*	1872	*
Employed	1970	892	949	1002	1095	1026	1145	1080	1118*	1120*	1829	-
Agriculture	881										1218	-
Mining		382	335	315	264	249	216	200	174*	170*		
Manufacturing	405	634	570	538	494	456	430	516	434*	455*	162	-
Others	683	7	22	32	38	46	51	59	54*	49*	500	-
Unemployed	-	0.4	1.2	1.7	2.0	2.6	2.8	3.3	3.0*	2.7*	43	47
Unemployment rate (%)	-										2.5	2.6
Production (thousand metric tons: calendar year)												
Agriculture, crop year												
1 Seed cotton	826	515	524	531	412	210	175	183	169	180	453	516
2 Wheat	153	156	159	182	174	548	559	500	483	550	489	701
3 Potatoes	181	167	147	134	112	108	128	175	240	303	308	357
4 Cotton (lint)	247	174	180	167	130	120	104	108	103	107	123	-
5 Grapes	121	100	88	80	96	122	127	46	54	110	110	81
6 Rice	26	20	23	20	24	21	44	40	47	82	40	50
7 Barley	51	39	30	25	22	17	23	26	25	19	16	36
8 Maize	60	32	34	18	19	90	30	36	36	38	34	55
Mining												
1 Hard coal	313	214	174	106	34	14	9	8	9	9	10	27
2 Crude petroleum	100	57	49	32	24	26	26	19	19	18	16	16
3 Natural gas (Mn cu. m.)	93	72	49	33	39	47	42	32	36	40	52	33
Manufacturing												
1 Cement	1013	447	262	178	78	49	36	18	33	55	69	89
2 Wheat flour	756	628	667	360	304	271	322	417	341	307	315	293
3 Aluminium	380	345	252	237	237	198	189	196	229	269	289	-
Production indexes period	-	75.8	71.5	69.3	60.4	51.8	50.2	48.4	47.4	54.3	51.4	
averages	96.0	73.0	67.0	50.0	43.0	33.0	32.0	-	-	-	82.3	54

Item	1991	1992	1993	1994	1995	1996	1997	1998	1999	2000	2001	2002
Agriculture (1989 - 91 = 100)	96.0	73.0	66.0	40.0	41.0	29.8	26.6	28.1	31.7	-	41.3	-
Industry (1990 = 100)												-
Manufacturing (1990 = 100)												
Energy (annual values)	99	57	39	33	26	26	26	19	19	18	16	16
Crude petroleum ('000 m. t.)	-	-	-	-	-	-	-	-	-	-	3	-
Production	-	-	-	-	-	-	-	-	-	-	-	-
Exports	-	-	-	-	-	-	-	-	-	-	-	-
Imports												
Consumption												
Coal ('000 m.t.)	313	214	174	106	34	20	17	19	19	22	24	36
Production	274	186	80	42	-	14	219	-	60	-	-	-
Exports	649	422	33	14	-	-	-	-	-	-	5	-
Imports	688	450	127	78	-	-	-	-	-	-	1	-
Consumption												
Natural gas (Mn cu. m.)	93	72	49	33	39	47	42	32	36	40	52	33
Production	-	-	-	-	-	-	-	-	-	-	-	-
Exports	2	1	1	1	1	1	2	1	1	1	565	486
Imports	-	-	-	-	-	-	-	-	-	-	-	-
Consumption												
Electricity (mn kWh)	17,600	16,800	17,700	17,000	14,800	14,980	14,005	14,422	15,797	14,247	14,382	15,244
Production	5400	5600	6400	5800	4200	4890	4247	3724	3831	3909	4047	3874
Exports	6900	6400	5200	4900	4900	3978	4345	3969	3641	5242	5396	4659
Imports	19,100	17,600	16,500	16,100	15,500	14,068	14,103	14,667	15,607	15,580	15,731	16,029
Consumption												

Note

* ADB internal estimates

Source: Asian Development Bank (2002c and 2003).

Since its disintegration from the FSU, it has experienced a significant fall in the production of agricultural, industrial and manufacturing output. As shown in Table 1.10 agricultural output (1989-91=100), fell from 75.8 in 1992 to 54.0 in 2002. Likewise industrial output (1990=100) dropped from 96.0 in 1991 to 82.3 in 2001 while manufacturing output (1990=100) declined from 96 to 41 in the same period. This fall in output has significantly increased unemployment and poverty in the country. While official figures indicate unemployment rate to be about 3%, unofficial estimates suggest as high as 40% people are unemployed.

High unemployment together with a fall in national output has contributed to a high level of poverty in Tajikistan. Poverty is widespread in the country. About 80% of the population live below the poverty line,[3] which has significantly increased its reliance on external debt. External debt as percentage of GDP increased from 73% in 1990 to 97% in 2001 (Table 1.10). Appendix II presents socio-economic indicators of Tajikistan.

Tajikistan primarily relies on the exports of a few commodities, namely cotton and aluminium, making its economy highly vulnerable to external shocks. These two commodities together contribute over 70% of export earnings. Most of its petroleum and gas requirements are being met through imports from Uzbekistan, while it exports electricity to Uzbekistan. It is estimated that the drugs trade accounts for about 50 percent of the economy. Rising tension between Tajikistan and its neighbouring countries appears to be partly due to drug trafficking that takes place through its territories. The World Bank Institute governance indicators reported in Table 1.11 suggest that Tajikistan has weak institutions and governance. In 2001, it ranked below the tenth percentile in all key governance measures except 'voice and accountability' in which it ranked in the 27th percentile (Gleason, 2003).

High unemployment and rising poverty have significantly increased reliance on external debt in both Kyrgyzstan and Tajikistan. By mid 2001, Kyrgyz Republic's external debt was 110% of GDP (which was 33% of GDP in 1993), while that of Tajikistan was 97%. These levels are extremely high and unsustainable without significant improvements in export earnings. In this context, and also in the context of employment creation, international integration is crucial for these countries. However, there are several stumbling blocks in their attempts towards international integration including cumbersome customs and border formalities, weak institutions and poor physical infrastructure. These

[3]The World Bank estimates suggest that since independence Tajikistan's per capita income declined by 85%. It fell from US$ 1,050 in 1990 to US$ 150 by 2000. In the same period pensioners' income dropped from US$ 70 to US$ 2 (World Bank, 2003)

contribute to higher costs, making their products uncompetitive in international markets.

Table 1.11. World Bank Institute Governance Indicators for Tajikistan

Governance indicator	Year	Percentile rank (0-100) in %	Estimate (-2.5 to +2.5)	Standard deviation	Number of surveys/ polls
Voice and accountability	2000/01	27.6	-0.69	0.19	3
Political stability/No violence	2000/01	3.1	-1.77	0.42	2
Government effectiveness	2000/01	7.5	-1.31	0.28	3
Regulatory quality	2000/01	5.9	-1.46	0.38	3
Rule of law	2000/01	4.7	-1.25	0.22	4
Control of corruption	2000/01	9.3	-1.08	0.24	3

Source: Gleason (2003)

Geographic location and distance to international markets cannot be changed. But man-made distortions can definitely be removed, which can help create an appropriate business climate. According to an estimate, transportation costs as well as official and unofficial charges in the Central Asian land-locked countries, can be as high as 50% of the value of the consignment (Molnar and Ojala, 2003), which is much higher than what other land-locked developing countries in South Asia incur. For example, transportation costs and other charges that Bhutan and Nepal incur are about 20% of the value of the goods (Sharma, 1999). Consequently, the Central Asian countries are less attractive for the private sector, including foreign investment. High transportation costs deter export-oriented activities which are employment intensive and which need to acquire input at lower costs and supply output on time.

Together with other Central Asian countries, Kyrgyzstan and Tajikistan are land-locked. Goods imported from, or exported to, outside Commonwealth of Independent States (CIS) countries have to pass through neighbouring countries' territories. Since tariff structure varies between the countries in the region, there is an incentive for smuggling of imported goods from the low tariff to the high tariff country(ies). To prevent this, each country has stringent border and customs formalities, which are not managed in a transparent way. Goods are checked in several locations and traders are required to fill in several forms at entry and exit borders and pay official and unofficial charges. These man-made distortions have significantly delayed international integration of the Central Asian countries, but most effected countries by these distortions are Kyrgyz Republic and Tajikistan. The present study aims to investigate development challenges faced by these countries which are equally relevant to other countries in the region. Their experience can also provide useful lessons to other developing countries which are in the path of global integration.

This book is structured into six chapters. Following this introduction, Chapter 2 presents an analytical framework within which we discuss the experiences of Kyrgyzstan and Tajikistan. Chapter 3 assesses policy framework, while trade performance is discussed in Chapter 4. Chapter 5 discusses development challenges. Policy recommendations are presented in Chapter 6.

Chapter 2

TRADE AND DEVELOPMENT: THEORY AND EMPIRICAL EVIDENCE

INTRODUCTION

The traditional neoclassical trade models assert that outward-orientation results in higher production and consumption, generating welfare gains. These 'static gains' mainly come from specialization. However, there are several 'dynamic gains' from trade such as greater competition, access to superior technology and productivity improvement. In recent years, these gains have received growing attention (Romer, 1986). Some economists, such as Krugman (1994), argue that dynamic gains are more important to sustain development in the long run. When the static and dynamic gains are combined, the total gains from trade are much higher (Havrylyshyn, 1990).

The purpose of this chapter is to establish the link between trade, growth and development using both theoretical and empirical work[4]. The chapter is organised as follows: The analytical framework is discussed in the next section followed by the literature reviewed and an international comparison of productivity growth that emerges from an outward-oriented strategy. These discussions will provide a framework for the analysis of Kyrgyzstan and Tajikistan in later chapters.

---

[4] This chapter draws heavily on Sharma (1999).

ANALYTICAL FRAMEWORK

Until the 1980s, protection of domestic industries, in the form of high tariffs and quantitative restrictions (QRs) such as import quotas and licenses, was widely considered to be the best way to achieve the political and economic goals in least developed countries (LDCs)[5]. First, protection helps to develop a variety of import-substitution (IS) industries. Second, financing development via tariffs, import quotas and licenses is considered politically more attractive as they provide a tool to political leaders to tax consumers in a hidden manner (Corden, 1987). However, a high level of protection acts as a tax on exports by appreciating the real exchange rate, leading to a lower level of exports. As exports decline and a shortage of foreign exchange emerges further restrictions are introduced. This forces domestic industries either not to utilise their full capacity or to use locally produced intermediate inputs and capital goods[6], leading to lower levels of production and exports (Little et al., 1970; Bhagwati and Desai, 1970).

Furthermore, QRs encourage black marketing of imported goods as they provide an attractive premium, leading to the shift of resources toward directly unproductive profit-seeking activities (DUP) rather than productive activities[7]. There is also a tendency to hold excessive inventories due to long delays in obtaining import licences and frequent changes in regulations. The lengthy licensing and custom formalities force firms to hire additional employees to perform such duties and frequently to bribe government officials. Furthermore, excessive profits facilitated by the protection from external competition induces managerial slack[8], while the small size of domestic market does not allow large scale production and efficient utilization of resources. Thus, productivity growth is lower in a protective regime (Little et al., 1970; Bhagwati, 1978; Krueger, 1978). Figure 2.1 explains how restrictions may retard overall growth.

[5] Tariffs are less damaging than the QRs, because the former at least permits competition over time as movements in world prices are reflected in domestic prices, while the latter do not. Furthermore, QRs also lead to monopoly profits.

[6] The experiences of India and many other LDCs have confirmed that inputs produced locally under the IS strategy are often neither competitive in price nor in quality. Thus, industries using these inputs incur a higher cost burden.

[7] See Bhagwati (1982) and Bhagwati and Srinivashan (1988). DUP refers to those activities which constitute "unproductive" ways of making an income, in that entrepreneurs use resources to produce income (or profit) but no socially valued output.

[8] Rodrik (1992a), however, argues that similar logic can also be applied to the export-oriented strategy. Excessive profits in the export-oriented industries may lead entrepreneurs towards the 'easy life'.

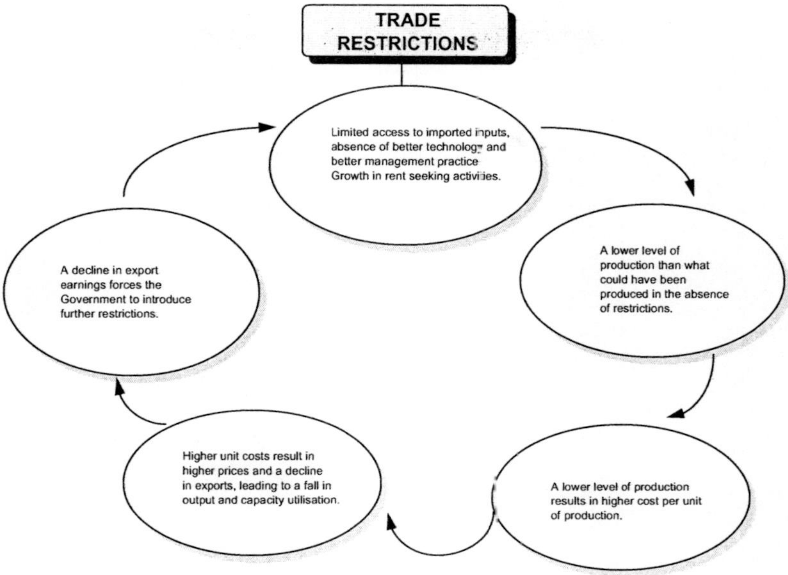

Figure 2.1. Vicious Circle of Trade Restrictions and Inward-orientation

The inward-oriented policy also creates an environment for rent seeking. To evade tariffs and import more than the approved quantity, imports are often under-invoiced as these items carry a high premium. Exports too are under-invoiced to sell foreign currencies in the black markets unless export subsidies are far greater than the return from the black marketing of foreign currencies. If export subsidies are greater than the return from the black marketing of foreign currencies, then the exports are over-invoiced. Thus, an inward-oriented strategy uses resources to produce profits rather than socially valued output. Figure 2.2 demonstrates the effects of trade restrictions on production and resource allocation.

A'B' is the production possibilities curve (PPC) of a country which shows the maximum limit of commodities X (exportable) and Y (IS product) that can be produced in the absence of distortions. Supposing that this nation enjoys a comparative advantage in commodity X. In the absence of restrictions, the relative commodity price would be determined at P which determines the optimum level of production. At this price it produces more of commodity X and less of commodity Y. By exchanging X for Y society ends up consuming at the highest indifference curve i.e., IC_{III}.

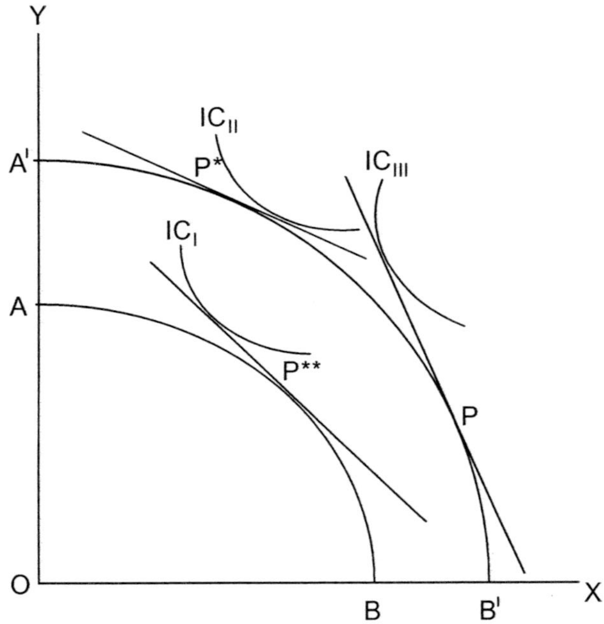

Source: Adopted from Kirkpatrick and Weiss (1992) with some modifications

Figure 2.2. Effects of Trade Restrictions on Production and Resource Allocation

Now assume that the government has introduced tariffs and QRs on the imports of commodity Y and the tariff inclusive price is P*. Since Y is a protected sector, it attracts resources away from X (export-oriented sector), leading to a decline in exportable production, which is typically a labour intensive sector in developing countries. Furthermore, there may be a considerable amount of managerial slack in the protected sector.

The decline in exportable production (commodity X) on the one hand, and the higher prices for the locally produced IS good (commodity Y) on the other hand, result in a lower level of welfare as the nation now consumes at a lower indifferent curve IC_{II}. Frequently the more significant cost of trade restrictions is seen because of the loss of potential output either due to rent seeking behaviour to receive preferential treatment or to the negative incentive effects of protection which induce x-inefficiency. These effects can push the PPC inward from A'B' to AB (Kirkpatrick and Weiss, 1992). This results in a further decline in welfare as society now consumes at a lowest indifference curve i.e., IC_{I}. Thus, the gap between A'A and B'B shows a loss in production caused by protection.

In contrast, an outward-oriented liberal strategy, by minimising rent seeking activities and increasing access to imported intermediate inputs and the best technology, leads to higher productivity growth (Krugman, 1987; Dornbusch, 1992). Even though these gains of outward-orientation are difficult to measure they play a significant role in economic growth. As Bhagwati (1988) points out factors which cannot be quantified are not necessarily unimportant in economics.

A movement from inward-orientation to outward-orientation brings several benefits. First, outward-oriented strategy provides an opportunity for exporting to new markets and thereby enables the country to enjoy the benefits of economies of scale, especially when the size of the domestic market is small. When exports expand, domestic industries that supply intermediate inputs to the exporting sector will benefit from an increased demand for their products. Even if most inputs are imported, export growth would create extra demand for labour and various types of services, e.g., banks, shipping, and workshops etc. In addition to this, diffusion of technological knowledge and increased availability of trained labour and management lead to an improvement in productivity of non-export activities. It is frequently assumed that in developing countries foreign trade is a channel through which embodied and disembodied technology are introduced and diffused (Hsia, 1987). Furthermore, export expansion relaxes the foreign exchange constraint and ensures regular supplies of intermediate inputs and equipment, leading to an improvement in capacity utilization[9].

Second, an outward-oriented policy creates competition and forces domestic firms to adopt best technology. Furthermore, it also encourages innovation. But equally, Schumpeterian's arguments suggest that the opposite might also be the case (Bhagwati, 1988). In addition, exposure to foreign firms improves the management practices and the skills of labour force.

Third, a liberal trade regime also has an advantage in absorbing new ideas generated in the rest of the world. When a country adopts an outward-oriented policy it benefits from learning by doing. Lewis (1955) argues that countries which are open will have an advantage in absorbing technological innovations developed in advanced nations and concludes:

> New ideas will be accepted more rapidly in those societies where people are accustomed to change. A country which is isolated, is by contrast unlikely to absorb new ideas quickly (Lewis, 1955, p.178).

---

[9] In LDCs, where eighty percent of imports consist of intermediate inputs and capital goods, the foreign exchange constraint substantially reduces the levels of production and productivity in manufacturing (Ostery, 1991; Thomas, 1989; Esfahani, 1991).

Fourth, an outward-oriented strategy discourages DUP and rent-seeking activities. But, it is equally possible that if the country pursuing a liberalization program has a long open border with its neighbours then liberalization may increase smuggling, if the neighbours have an inward-looking strategy (Rodrik, 1992a). In this situation liberalization increases rent seeking. Figure 2.3 explains a possible positive link between outward-orientation and productivity growth.

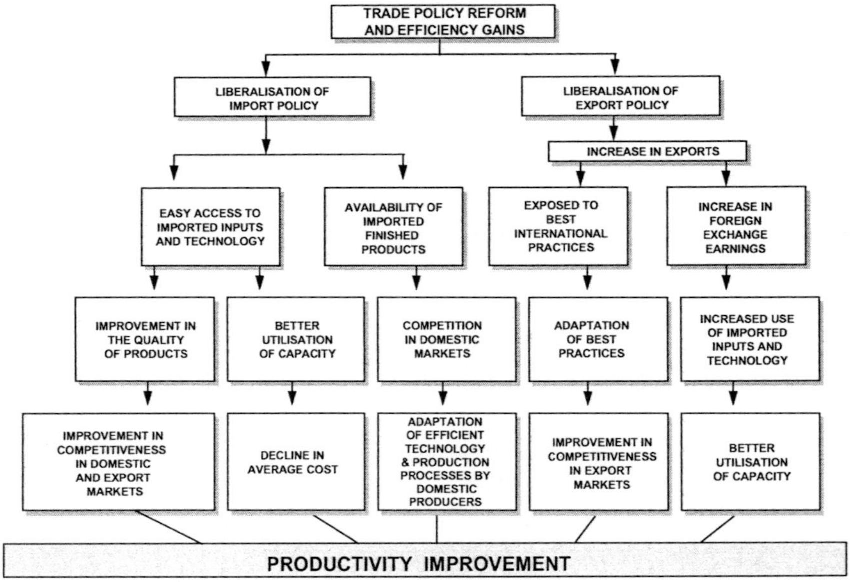

Figure 2.3. Link Between Openness and Productivity Growth

Rodrik (1992a, 1992b), however, argues that there are no theoretical reasons to believe that protection discourages productivity improvement. He argues that protection can in fact improve efficiency by increasing domestic output and market share. It is import liberalization that retards productivity growth by shrinking the domestic firm's sales and reducing incentives to invest in technological effort. He notes that:

> The larger is the market served by the domestic firm, the higher will be the marginal benefit of technological effort. This is because the benefit of cost reductions is proportional to the level of output. Consequently, any liberalization that lowers domestic output will harm technological effort. (Rodrik, 1992b, p. 101)

It has been argued that in LDCs a liberalization program is often less effective due to market failures and barriers to entry and exit. For example, the labour market is distorted either due to the lack of appropriate training programs or regulations such as minimum wage policy and employment conditions. Besides this, the secondary market in capital equipment is not well developed in these economies. Thus, despite liberalization a loss making firm may not exit until prices fall below the average variable cost and may not exit, with the exception of a natural exit, if they are cross-subsidised by affiliates in other business (Rodrik, 1992c).

Doubts have also been expressed as to whether privatization and liberalization policies will bring about any improvement in efficiency because of the low supply elasticities and the early stage of industrialization in LDCs (Stein, 1992; Mosley, 1993). Supply elasticities may be low due to excessive market concentration, infrastructure bottlenecks, or a lack of institutions. Thus, whether outward-oriented liberal strategies really improve efficiency in LDCs which is a key to succeed is ambiguous on theoretical grounds alone and must be examined empirically. Bhagwati notes that:

> Although the arguments for the success of the export promotion strategy based on economies of scale and X-efficiency are plausible, empirical support for them is not available (Bhagwati, 1988, p. 39).

On the other hand, Pack observes:

> To date there is no clear confirmation of the hypothesis that countries with an external orientation benefit from greater growth in technical efficiency in component sectors of manufacturing (Pack, 1988, p. 353).

Since our objective is to shed light on trade and development challenges of newly independent states, we began our analysis first by reviewing the literature on trade-orientation and the performance of manufacturing output, exports and employment. Next, the literature on trade-orientation and productivity growth is analysed.

Trade-Orientation and Manufacturing Growth Performance

A large number of studies have examined the link between outward-orientation and the performance of manufacturing. This includes both country studies and cross-country studies. The former have concluded that restrictions prevent growth in the following manner[10]: First, they distort resource allocation away from a nation's comparative advantage and hence reduce output and exports by attracting resources towards the production of protected products. Second, as restricted trade regimes impart a home market bias, the benefits of economies of scale are lost due to the small size of the domestic market. Thus, industries which require a large scale operation to be efficient will not be developed or will operate inefficiently. Even if these industries are established their capacity can not be utilised fully due to the small size of the domestic market. Hence, the net effect of this bias is to discourage greater economies of scale and the full utilization of installed capacity. Third, restricted trade regimes typically create a shortage of foreign exchange which impedes the use of imported inputs and technology required for production of exportable. Thus, country studies have suggested that restricted trade regimes hinder growth in manufacturing output, exports and employment, while trade policy reforms can stimulate their growth.

Cross-country studies have explored the link between trade-orientation and the performance of manufacturing. An early attempt was made in a study undertaken by the United Nations Conference on Trade and Development (UNCTAD) in 1969, using data from 53 developing countries. In that study, manufactured exports per capita were regressed on: (i) the availability of natural resources, approximated by the per capita agrable land, (ii) a certain level of manufacturing production, approximated by the percentage share of population employed in manufacturing, (iii) the country's ability to attract foreign investment and foreign aid, proxied by the inflow of per capita foreign aid, and (iv) the membership of a preferential trade area. The regression results suggested that the availability of natural resources is negatively related with the manufacturing export performance, while the other independent variables have a positive impact. The study argues that explanatory variable (iii) indirectly captures the effect of policy regime and concludes that outward-orientation results in higher exports. However, it should be noted that the inflow of per capita foreign aid is not an appropriate proxy for capturing the effect of the policy regime.

In a similar inquiry, Mahfuzur Rahman (1973) regresses the manufactured export performance of developing countries on: (i) the absolute size of the manufacturing sector, approximated by the share of manufacturing in GDP, (ii) level of industrialization, measured by the share of manufacturing in GDP, (iii) degree of manufactured export diversification which is expressed by a Gini

[10] The important country studies examining the link between trade-orientation and growth are: Little et al. (1970), Balassa (1971,1982), Bhagwati (1978), Bhagwati and Desai (1970), Krueger (1978) and Papageorgiou et al. (1991).

coefficient, (iv) number of export markets, measured by a Gini coefficient, (v) corrected Gini coefficient for market concentration as it does not take into account the size of the markets and the geographical distance between trade partners, and (vi) the index of outward orientation, proxied by the number of export flows, defined as the export of any one manufactured product to any one foreign market. Using data on export flows from 37 developing countries to 11 developed countries, he regresses these explanatory variables separately against the dependent variable i.e., the value of manufactured exports. The regression results for the first five variables are not strong, while the index of outward-orientation is highly significant. This led him to conclude that trade-orientation of a country determines the volume of its manufactured exports rather than the size of the manufacturing sector or any other explanatory variables included in the model. However, these results must be interpreted with caution given that they were obtained using several bivariate regressions and lacked strong theoretical justification. Similar results were recorded in a study by UNIDO (1974).

Using data from 45 developing countries Morrison (1976a) examines the factors that influence manufactured exports from these countries. Like Mahfuzur Rahman (1973), he develops a model by including both the supply side and policy related factors; he argues that trade liberalization in developed nations can only increase export intensity in developing countries if they are able to raise their production (supply). The supply side variables included in his model are: (i) size of the domestic market, (ii) level of economic development, (iii) natural resource endowment and (iv) availability of skilled labour force; while included policy related variables are: (i) level of protection, (ii) rate of inflation, and (iii) export promotion programs. The regression results show that export performance is positively related to the level of development (measured as GDP per capita), natural resource endowment (measured in terms of population density) and the degree of openness (measured as a share of imported goods in total consumption of manufactured goods). The levels of inflation and skilled labour had no significant impact on the exports of manufactured goods. However, he could not construct a proxy for export promotion schemes and hence it was not included in the final estimated model. Morrison argues that the level of development and the natural resource endowment are not essential prerequisites for successful export performance. He asserts that the more developed countries could export sophisticated products, while the relatively less developed countries could export the less sophisticated or traditional products.

Chenery (1980) designs an open input-output model to explain the sources of industrialization. He specifies the following variables as likely to influence industrialization in an economy: (i) expansion of domestic demand, (ii) expansion of exports, (iii) import substitution, and (iv) changes in intermediate demand. Using historical data over the post war period for Korea, Taiwan, Turkey, Mexico, Yugoslavia, Colombia and Japan, he found that the first three variables could explain about 80 percent of the rising share of manufacturing in an economy. The relative contribution of each of these variables was highly influenced by the role of international trade in a country. He concludes that to increase the share of manufacturing in GDP in the long run, trade policy would have to be export-oriented. The remainder of about 20% is due to technological change, as measured by an expansion of the demand for intermediate goods. Chenery found that the relative contribution of technological change to the expansion of heavy industry is substantially higher than it is to the expansion of light industry.

Balassa (1978) using different ratios and the Spearman rank correlation coefficient, based on data for 11 countries, examines the link between exports and output growth and the impact of export growth on the structure of the manufacturing sector. He finds that Singapore, Korea and Taiwan experienced dramatic increases in their total exports, including manufactured exports and the export-output ratios during 1960-66 as a result of trade policy reforms which took place in the early 1960s. Despite their poor natural resource endowment, these three countries also made remarkable progress in primary exports and hence in total exports compared to Argentina, Brazil and Mexico which had not fully liberalized their factor and commodity markets.

Greenaway and Nam (1988) using a number of qualitative and quantitative criteria, based on data for 41 countries, examine the various features of industrialization. The countries that pursued an outward-oriented policy achieved higher growth in manufacturing output, exports, employment and are less vulnerable to external shocks. They also observed lower incremental capital output ratios (ICORs) in these countries. Finally, Krueger (1978) and Bhagwati (1978), in multi-country studies, find that trade restrictions lead to excess capacity and excess inventory build up which lead to higher ICORs, while liberalization results in efficient utilization of capacity and hence lower ICORs[11].

In a multi-country study Krueger (1983) observes that trade liberalization not only increases manufacturing output and exports but also creates more employment opportunities, leading to a more equitable income distribution. She concludes that export production in LDCs is typically more labour intensive than import-substitution and hence export expansion creates more employment. This

[11] ICORs are a popular measure of efficiency in policy analysis, which refer to the amount of capital per unit of output. However, it should be noted that they are not good measures of overall efficiency because they measure only the relation of capital to output, leaving out the contribution of intermediate inputs and labour to output.

finding is similar to Banerji and Riedel (1980) who found more rapid employment and output growth in Taiwan which pursued an outward-oriented strategy than in India - a country with a restrictive trade regime. Since the primary and manufacturing activities are labour intensive in LDCs, reducing tariffs would create additional employment in both activities (Balassa, 1982). Bourguignon and Morrison (1989), through the study of a sample of 37 developing countries, conclude that trade restrictions increase income inequality and leads to a drop of four to five percentage points in the income of poorest population. The findings of Krueger (1983), and Bourguignon and Morrison (1989) are in line with the predictions of the Stolper-Samuelson theorem that free trade benefits the relatively abundant factor of production, which in most LDCs is labour.

In a study of high performing Asian countries, World Bank (1993) examines the link between openness and growth. Multiple regression analysis for the 1960 to 1985 period covering about fifty countries indicated that GDP and productivity growth are significantly correlated with the average share of manufactured exports. The share of manufactured exports was higher in those countries that successfully pursued an outward-oriented industrialization. However, the impact of manufactured exports share in GDP growth was smaller in comparison with the other determinants of growth such as: a country's GDP relative to the US in 1960 (a measure of relative income level), rate of primary enrolment in 1960 and the average share of investment in GDP. When productivity growth is being explained, manufactured export shares seem to be more important.

Trade-Orientation and Productivity Growth

In this section we review the literature on trade-orientation and manufacturing productivity growth in developing countries. As discussed in Chapter 1, the debate has produced a large number of country and cross-country studies. Thus, the analysis is presented into two sub-sections.

Cross-Country Studies

Cross-country studies have made statistical comparisons to see if differences in productivity growth are related to differences in trade policies. These studies have shown that, in the outward-oriented economies, as exports expand, both the resource allocation and external effects lead to economy-wide productivity and output growth. There are at least two theoretical explanations for this correlation. One emphasises the benefits of economies of scale, while the other emphasises x-efficiency or competition.

In a comparison of productivity performance of Israel's and Philippine's industries with that of the US, Pack (1984a) finds a lower total factor productivity (TFP) growth in the former countries which pursued protectionist policies. The productivity performance of the US industries, which pursued an outward-oriented policy, was superior. Bergsman (1974) calculates losses in x-efficiency caused by protectionist policies in Brazil (6.8%), Malaysia (0.4%), Mexico (2.2%), Pakistan (5.4%), Norway (2%) and Philippines (2.6%). He concludes that:

> Open economies show the lowest costs of misallocation. The costs of misallocation seem to be lower in larger and more industrialised countries and higher in countries with smaller domestic markets for protected production (Bergsman, 1974, p. 420).

Nishimizu and Robinson (1984) compare manufacturing productivity growth in Korea (1960-77), Turkey (1963-76), Yugoslavia (1965-78) and Japan (1955-73). They observed higher productivity growth in Korea and Japan which pursued an outward-oriented strategy than in Turkey and Yugoslavia which had an inward-oriented development strategy. Despite differences in productivity growth across the four countries, they all observed higher productivity in heavy industries and lower productivity in light industries. They found that if the sources of growth are decomposed as being attributable to 'export expansion' and 'import-substitution', the variation in productivity growth suggests that export expansion leads to higher TFP growth through economies of scale and/or through competition, while import substitution results in lower TFP growth.

In a sample of developed countries during the interwar period, Verdoorn (1949) found that output growth was positively correlated with productivity growth. This led him to conclude that there is a link between economies of scale and productivity gains which is known as 'Verdoorn's Law'. Batchelor et al. (1980) using cross-country data confirm this finding for a set of countries for the period 1964-71. Kaldor (1967) finds that while 'Verdoorn's Law' holds strongly in the manufacturing and construction sectors, it does not hold in any other sector. Balassa (1967) argues that cost reductions or productivity improvement in one industry will have a cumulative effect on the manufacturing sector as a whole through input-output linkages and through the effects of higher incomes on the demand for goods.

Nishimizu and Page (1990) in a cross-country study of 17 countries, which includes both developed and developing countries, investigate the links between trade policy, market-orientation and productivity growth. Given data limitations, the periods covered varies from country to country. However, they broadly cover the period from the late 1950s/early 1960s to the late 1970s/early 1980s. The whole period is divided into two sub-periods: (i) the periods prior to the first oil shock (through 1973), and (ii) the periods following 1973 up to the early 1980s. TFP growth is regressed on: 'export demand', 'import demand' and 'total domestic demand'. The model also includes QRs and non-market allocation of resources[12]. The model was estimated using panel data for the entire period and for the two important sub-periods of interest. Results indicated that export growth is positively related to TFP growth only in those economies that do not rely much on QRs and follow the market-oriented strategies. This was true in both sub-periods, but stronger before the first oil crisis. They found a negative relationship between import penetration and TFP growth, especially in the open market economies in the second period, but not in the first period. Industries protected through QRs seem to have difficulty adjusting to external shocks, unlike industries operating in the open market environment.

Young (1995) compares TFP growth in South Korea, Hong Kong, Taiwan and Singapore. Estimates are provided for the whole economy as well as for the manufacturing, services and other industries. Given the difficulty in obtaining data, the period covered varies, but broadly covers the period between 1966 to 1990. He observed an average annual decline of 1.0% in manufacturing productivity in Singapore during 1970-90, while in Korea and Taiwan it grew at 3.0% and 1.7% per annum (p.a.) during 1966-90 respectively. Rapid growth in manufacturing output and GDP was mainly brought about by factor accumulation, while the contribution of TFP growth was very small in all the countries. Factor accumulation increased mainly due to a rise in participation rates, education levels and investment (with the exception of Hong Kong).

In a comparison of productivity performance in 41 developing countries, the IMF (1992a) reports that the outward-oriented countries achieved significantly higher growth in GDP and productivity than countries that pursued inward-oriented trade policies during 1975-89. However, the study did not spell out the methodology applied. A similar analysis was done by the World Bank (1987), based on the work of Chenery and others (1986), which concluded that the more outward-oriented the trade regime is, the greater is the contribution of TFP growth to GDP growth. For example, in Hong Kong and Korea, TFP growth contributed 42 and 47% to GDP growth respectively, while in the least outward-orientated countries its share was much lower (about 23%).

---

[12] They have, however, not discussed how these variables were measured.

Country Studies

Although cross-country analyses have established a strong link between outward-orientation and productivity growth, in case study type analyses of individual country experiences this link is not robust. For example, Tsao (1985) in a study of Singapore's manufacturing sector finds that TFP growth for the three-digit sub-sector was eight-tenths of one percent during the 1970s, with 17 out of 28 sub-sectors showed negative TFP growth. Furthermore, output growth was mainly brought about by factor accumulation, while the contribution of TFP growth was less than 10%. Besides data inaccuracies, Tsao suspects that the predominance of foreign investment, a low wage policy and the lack of indigenous entrepreneurs may have resulted in a low level of innovation and hence poor productivity growth. Chenery and others (1986) also finds a lower level of TFP growth for Singapore for the post-1960 period and concludes that the rapid increase in capital stock may have caused the slow change in TFP (cited in Balassa 1988).

Krueger and Tuncer (1982) provide TFP growth estimates for the Turkish manufacturing industries during 1963-1976[13]. Based on the nature of trade and payment regime, the whole period is divided into four sub-periods: (i) 1963-67 was a relatively relaxed period, (ii) 1967-70 was the period of growing restrictions, (iii) 1970-73 was the period of relaxed trade and payment regimes following a devaluation, and (iv) 1973-76 was a period of growing restrictions. They observed a higher TFP growth when the Turkish trade regime was relatively open and a lower TFP growth when the trade regime was somewhat restrictive. Furthermore, there was no tendency among the highly protected industries to improve their productivity and the government owned industries exhibited lower productivity growth than the private sector industries. Krueger and Tuncer, however, do not undertake an econometric analysis to test these hypotheses. During the whole period of analysis, TFP grew at 2.10% per annum, contributing about 17% to output growth. Their estimates were based on gross output terms.

Kim (1994) estimates TFP growth for manufacturing industries in Korea for 1967-88. During this period TFP grew at an average annual rate of about 2%, contributing about 11% to output growth. He then regresses TFP growth on capacity utilization, economies of scale, export-orientation, net exports, import liberalization, industrial concentration, effective rate of protection (ERP) and research and development (RandD). Although it was expected that import liberalization would have a positive impact on TFP growth, the link was found to

[13] Printing and publishing, and miscellaneous manufacturing were excluded from the analysis in the absence of appropriate deflators.

be statistically insignificant. The author explains that this may have resulted from the fact that even if import liberalization contributes to industrial efficiency, it raises the ratio of imports to gross output, which is negatively related to TFP. The effect of a rise in ERP on TFP growth, as expected, turned out to be negative and statistically significant, while the export-orientation variable was not statistically significant. When the export-orientation variable was changed to the net export/output ratio, it became positive and statistically significant, but no strong reason is given for using the net export/output ratio. No statistical evidence was found that TFP growth is influenced by changes in capacity utilization and the degree of industrial concentration. A strong association was observed between the economies of scale and TFP growth.

Kwon (1986) estimates TFP growth for the Korean manufacturing during 1961-78 which is divided into the two sub-periods: (i) 1961-72 and (ii) 1972-78. The former sub-period represents the 'self-sustaining growth' period, while the latter was the period of 'transition towards heavy industries'. TFP growth estimates, based on gross output terms, indicate 1.79 and 4.8% annual growth in the earlier and the latter sub-periods respectively. Linking productivity growth to key parameters of the cost function, TFP growth was decomposed into: (i) technical change, (ii) non-constant returns to scale, and (iii) changes in capacity utilization. The analysis showed that about 20% of TFP growth in the earlier sub-period and about 5% in the latter sub-period was explained by an improvement in capacity utilization. This led Kwon to conclude that an improvement in capacity utilization is a source of TFP growth in LDCs which is too significant to be ignored.

Dollar and Sokoloff (1990) report a 6% annual growth in manufacturing productivity in Korea during 1963-79. They found a higher productivity in labour intensive than in capital intensive industries. A lower productivity growth in the latter was mainly attributed to the availability of subsidised capital for the heavy and chemical industries in 1970s. Econometric results indicated that TFP growth was positively related to the size of the industry (proxied by the number of employees)[14] and export growth. Their estimate, which is based on value added terms, is much higher than that of Kim (1994) and Kwon's (1986) estimates based on gross output terms.

Handoussa, Nishimizu and Page (1986) provide TFP growth estimates for 96 public sector manufacturing firms in Egypt during 1973-79. During this period Egypt experienced major changes in its policy environment. Based on the nature

[14] Note that this can be a misleading proxy when labour intensities differ greatly between industries. Thus, a relatively small labour intensive industry can be measured as being much larger than a large capital intensive industry.

of market orientation, these firms were grouped into export-oriented and import substitution. Results indicated that the former experienced an absolute fall in TFP growth (-1.91% p.a.), while the latter recorded an impressive growth in TFP (2.4% p.a.). The superior productivity performance of the import substitution firms was mainly attributed to increased access to imported inputs, leading to an improvement in capacity utilization. The poor productivity performance of the exported-oriented firms was attributed mainly to the closure of bilateral export markets for traditional exports. As a result there was a fall in output in these firms, leading to poor TFP growth. The econometric results supported the hypothesis that economies of scale (measured as output growth) is positively related to productivity growth.

Brown and Dominguez (1994) reports an average annual growth of 4.8% in manufacturing productivity in Mexico during 1984-90. During this period reforms were introduced in Mexico. Small scale firms involved in export activities (mostly with foreign participation) experienced a higher TFP growth. This indicates a link between foreign investment and TFP growth, which may have developed through the introduction of new technology, better work practices and improvement in the quality of work. Econometric results indicated that only GDP growth was positively linked to manufacturing productivity growth, while the coefficients of exports, imports and trade regime variables turned out to be insignificant.

Bonelli (1992) investigates the link between trade-orientation and manufacturing productivity growth in Brazil during 1975-85. The whole period is divided into two sub-periods based on the nature of policy regime: (i) 1975-80 and (ii) 1980-85. He found a lower TFP growth in the earlier sub-period when the trade regime was somewhat restrictive and an improvement in the latter sub-period when the trade regime was liberal. In the supply side analysis, TFP growth was explained by output growth in the both sub-periods, but the association was stronger in the liberalization period. When TFP growth was regressed on two demand side components, i.e. export expansion and import-substitution, the coefficients of both variables were statistically significant and positively related to TFP growth in the earlier sub-period, but not in the latter. When the model was estimated for the whole period, both export expansion and import-substitution variables were statistically significant and positively related to TFP growth.

Chen and Tang (1990) investigate the relation between TFP growth (estimated in gross output terms), output growth and export expansion using the two-digit manufacturing data from Taiwan for 1962-82. They found that in Taiwan, output growth has superior power in explaining productivity growth than export growth, even though export growth is the best way of achieving economies of scale, especially when the size of domestic market is small. In contrast, by examining the performance of export-oriented and import-substitution firms using data from 184 foreign firms in the Taiwanese electronic industry, Chen (1987) found that export-oriented firms are more efficient (6-11% closer to the production frontier) than the import-substitution firms. Furthermore, they also found that older firms tend to be more efficient than new firms.

Prim (1992) investigates the link between productivity growth and changes in economic policies using China's Jiangsu Province manufacturing industries data during 1953-88. He observed a substantial improvement in productivity in the early 1980s when reforms were introduced in China. The improvement in average productivity was largely due to relatively faster growth in collective industries than in state industries.

Perkins, Yuxing and Young (1993) estimate TFP growth for China's Xiamen economic zone industries for 1980-88. Based on the nature of the policy regime, the period of study is divided into the two sub-periods: (i) 1980-83 and (ii) 1984-88. In the earlier sub-period the policy environment was restrictive, but a substantial liberalization took place in the latter. Following liberalization, TFP grew from 4% to about 7% p.a. During the entire period of analysis, TFP grew at about 6% p.a. However, these results must be interpreted with some caution because how variables were measured for TFP growth estimates are not described. Econometric results, based on the panel data, indicate a higher TFP growth in joint venture and collective firms. Furthermore, capital intensity was negatively related to TFP growth, while the policy reforms had no significant impact on productivity growth. A dummy variable was used to capture the effects of policy reforms.

The World Bank (1993: 324-325) found that in Korea, the highly protected industries such as iron and steel had lower levels of TFP growth than the less protected industries like textile and clothing during 1966-85. The sectoral TFP growth rates of the Malaysian industries also showed a similar trend during 1973-89. TFP growth rates in protected sectors (such as noneletrical machinery, paper and paper products, iron and steel, and transport equipment) were lower than in a non-protected sector (namely textile and apparel). However, the experience of Japanese manufacturing does not show a similar trend. In Japan, a highly protected sector, the chemical and the metal working complex, in fact had an unusually higher rate of TFP growth between 1960-79. In short, the study did not find any clear relationship between the sectors protected and the level of TFP growth.

Kajiwara (1994) estimates TFP growth for the Philippines manufacturing sector during 1974-88. Based on the nature of trade regime, the period of study is divided into the two sub-periods: (i) 1974-79, and (ii) 1984-88. In the earlier sub-period, policy regime was very restrictive which was liberalized in the latter sub-period. In both sub-periods productivity (estimated in value added terms) declined, but somewhat controlled after the policy reforms (-3.5% vs -2.8% p.a.). In the post-reform period, only 3 out of 20 manufacturing sub-sectors recorded positive growth in productivity. Econometric results showed no significant link between import penetration and ERP. Furthermore, no significant relationship was observed between the level of ERP and TFP growth, and ERP and export-orientation. However, these results must be treated with caution as they were obtained from several bivariate regression equations (i.e., the dependent variable was separately regressed on a number of independent variables), rather than in a multivariate analytical framework.

Okuda (1994) estimates productivity growth for the manufacturing industries in Taiwan during 1978-91. The study period is divided into the two sub-periods: (i) 1978-1985, and (ii) 1986-91, based on the nature of policy regime. He found a marginal improvement in productivity growth in the latter sub-period when the policy regime was liberalized. Econometric investigations were carried out, using pooled data for the whole period. However, neither a time dummy was used nor were data split into the pre- and post-reform periods to capture the effects of changes in the policy environment. TFP indices, instead of TFP growth, were regressed[15] on: the ratio of foreign direct investment to total capital stock, export-orientation, import penetration and capital equipment per worker. Results indicated that sectors with higher foreign direct investment, lower capital intensity and less exposed to import competition were the sectors with higher productivity growth. However, a clear cut relationship between productivity growth and export-orientation was not observed.

Akrasanee and Wiboonchutikula (1994) estimate TFP growth for manufacturing industries in Thailand during 1963-86. They found that during this period TFP grew at 0.94% p.a., contributing only about 7% to output growth, while growth in factor inputs contributed about 93%[16]. They recorded higher TFP growth in export-oriented (EO) industries throughout the period, while import competing industries experienced a declining trend, especially in 1980s when the level of protection substantially fell.

Urata and Yokota (1994) examine the impact of a shift in policy environment on manufacturing productivity growth in Thailand during 1976-88. Based on the nature of the policy regime, the whole period is divided into the two sub-periods: (i) 1976-82 and (ii) 1982-88. The policy regime in the earlier sub-period was

[15] The author notes that when TFP growth was used as the dependent variable results were disappointing in terms of R^2 and the overall fit of the model was weak.

[16] Intermediate inputs and capital input grew more rapidly than the labour input.

somewhat restrictive, while a substantial liberalization took place in the latter. Results indicated a lower level of TFP growth following reforms despite an increase in output. Furthermore, in both sub-periods output growth was mainly brought about by factor accumulation as observed by Akrasane and Wiboonchutikula (1994). The contribution of TFP to output growth fell from about 27% in the restrictive period to about 6% in the liberalization period. However, these results must be treated with caution, given that the authors failed to report how factor inputs were measured or to justify the particular price indices used for TFP growth estimates. Econometric investigations were carried out by regressing TFP growth on output growth, ERP, domestic competitive pressure, RandD and the imported input ratio. In the pre-liberalization period, the coefficient of output growth was statistically significant and had a positive sign, while the coefficients of all other variables were statistically insignificant. However, in the post-reform period the coefficients of all independent variables were statistically significant and had expected signs.

Tybout, de Melo and Corbo (1991) report little improvement in manufacturing productivity in Chile following trade liberalization though they have not provided the actual estimates of TFP growth. They found that: (i) output per plant remained stable during 1967-79, (ii) value added per plant fell more rapidly than workers per plant, and (iii) value added per unit of capital fell substantially. Taking the last two items together they concluded that there was 'an unequivocal fall in manufacturing TFP during 1967-79'. They hypothesised that this may be due to unstable macro-economic conditions.

For Indian manufacturing, Goldar (1985) finds 1.31% annual growth in productivity during 1959-79, contributing about 18% to output growth. He observes a significant positive relationship between TFP and output growth and a significant negative relationship between TFP and import substitution. He finds that 1% higher growth in output was associated with about 0.5% higher growth in TFP. While a 10% higher contribution of import substitution was associated with about 0.6% lower annual growth rate in TFP.

In contrast, Ahluwalia (1991) reports 0.4% annual decline in TFP in Indian manufacturing industries during 1959/60-1985/86 - much lower than Golder (1985). Both estimates are based on value added terms. She notes that the average annual growth of 5.3% in value added was mainly achieved by factor accumulation and the contribution of TFP to value added was -7.5%. Ahluwalia (1991) argues that the Golder (1985) estimates were higher mainly due to differences in the coverage of the sectors; his data covered the large scale manufacturing sector, including electricity. Based on the nature of the policy regime, Ahluwalia (1991) divides the study period into the two sub-periods: (i)

1959/60-1979/80 and (ii) 1980/81-1985/86. The earlier sub-period was the period of inward-orientation, while the latter represents the period of outward-orientation. She finds negative productivity growth in the earlier period and an improvement in the latter period. She argues that poor TFP in the earlier sub-period was mainly due to excessive restrictions in trade and payment systems and a fall in infrastructure investment. Using panel data, econometric investigations were carried out for the two sub-periods. In the earlier sub-period, TFP growth was positively correlated with growth in value added, while the other independent variables, namely the number of firms in an industry, import-substitution, capital intensity and the scale effect (i.e., the stock of capital per factory), had no effect on productivity growth. However, in the latter sub-period, growth in value added and the scale effect were positively correlated with TFP growth, while capital intensity was negatively related to productivity growth. The coefficient for import-substitution and the number of firms within an industry were not statistically significant.

Fujita (1994) estimates of TFP growth for Indian manufacturing during 1981/82-1987/88 was -0.16% p.a. which is very close to the estimates of Ahluwalia (1991). The sources of data in both studies are the same, both cover almost the same period and use the same methodology. The marginal difference in results seems to be due to differences in the treatment of capital stock; Ahluwalia estimates capital stock using the perpetual inventory method, while Fujita uses the net capital formation data from the Annual Survey of Industries. Fujita observes a higher TFP growth in labour intensive industries than in capital intensive industries, but this observation was not statistically tested. Using several bivariate equations he finds: (a) a positive link between TFP growth and liberalization (proxied by the share of public enterprises), (b) a negative association between TFP growth and comparative advantage (proxied by capital-labour ratio), and (c) a positive link between growth in manufactured exports and TFP growth. However, these results should be interpreted with caution because the use of bivariate, rather than multivariate, equations in the analysis does not appear to be justified.

To sum up, with the exception of Chen and Tang (1990), Tsao (1985), Regmi (1994), Golder (1985) and Young (1995), all studies make an attempt to explain the link between outward-orientation and productivity growth. Except for Urata and Yokota (1994), a positive link between outward-orientation and productivity growth was observed in all studies. The cross-country studies generally found superior productivity performance in an outward-oriented economy than in an inward-oriented economy. With the exception of Young (1995), IMF (1992a), Krueger and Tuncer (1982), Pack (1984a), Kwon (1986), Prim (1992), World

Bank (1987 and 1993), Akrasanee and Wiboonchutikula (1994), and Tybout et al. (1991), all studies attempt to explain inter-industry variations in TFP growth in an econometric framework. But, with the exception of Harrison (1994), Nishimizu and Page (1990), and Nishimizu and Robinson (1984), none have applied the appropriate diagnostic tests such as tests for heteroscedasticity and the RESET test for specification error. The latter test is crucial especially when cross-sectional and pooled data are used. Hence the econometric results of these studies must be treated with caution.

CONCLUSION

Theoretical and empirical work discussed in this chapter reveals the following. First, following a shift to an outward-oriented strategy, there was an improvement in manufacturing output, exports and productivity in most cases. However, it is difficult to ascertain whether these improvements are brought about solely by the liberalization program or by other measures that generally follow a liberalization program or by the combination of these factors. None of the studies discriminates between the effects of trade policy and those of macro-economic policy. In practice, liberalization of trade has often accompanied liberalization in exchange control, banking sector reform and privatization. Rodrik (1992b) rightly observes that current terminology of outward-orientation and export promotion strategy lumps together macroeconomic policies with trade policy and credit for positive results is given solely to trade policy reform. Second, productivity growth estimates are sensitive to the methodology applied (gross output vs value added), treatment of capital stock and the price indices used. Thus, one should be careful when interpreting productivity growth estimates. Third, econometric results of the most studies are questionable due to data, variable measurement, model specification and estimation problems. Note that diagnostic tests, such as the tests for heteroscedasticity and the appropriateness of the functional form, while crucial in studies using panel and cross-sectional data, have been applied only in a few studies.

Chapter 3

POLICY DEVELOPMENT IN KYRGYZ REPUBLIC AND TAJIKISTAN

INTRODUCTION

The earlier chapter outlined how international integration facilitates trade and development, and accelerates growth in output, exports, employment and productivity. In this chapter our aim is to assess Kyrgyz Republic and Tajikistan's attempts towards global integration in a comparative perspective. Both countries have made attempts towards international integration, although the speed of integration varies between the countries. For instance, Kyrgyz Republic has been a fast reformer, while the reform process has been relatively slow in Tajikistan. In this chapter first we present an assessment of policy environment in Kyrgyz Republic followed by the assessment of Tajikistan's policy regime.

Kyrgyz Republic

Trade Policy Regime

Kyrgyz Republic is one of the most open economies in the region. It has reduced tariffs and subsidies, privatized state-owned enterprises (SOEs) and liberalized investment policies. Despite being a non-market economy for 70 years, these reforms enabled the Republic to become the first CIS country to join the WTO in 1998. After gaining the WTO membership it has further simplified its tariff structure and reduced tariff rates. The average tariff rates fell from 9.3 % in 1999 to 5.1% by 2002, a tariff rate similar to that of the developed world. Table

3.1 compares overall restrictiveness of trade policy in 15 BOR countries which shows that among the CIS countries both Kyrgyz Republic and Tajikistan have one of the least restrictive trade regimes in the region.

Table 3.1. A Comparative Perspective of Trade Restrictiveness in BOR Countries 1999 and 2002

	1999		2002	
	Average Tariff	Overall Rating/1	Average Tariff	Overall Rating /1
Armenia	3.7	1.0	4.0	1.0
Azerbaijan	12.0	5.0	10.8	2.0
Belarus	12.6	8.0	12.2	8.0
Estonia	0.0	1.0	3.1	1.0
Georgia	10.0	2.0	10.9	2.0
Kazakhstan	7.8	4.0	7.8	4.0
Kyrgyz Republic	9.2	1.0	5.1	1.0
Latvia	5.3	1.0	4.3	1.0
Lithuania	4.5	1.0	5.3	1.0
Moldova	8.9	1.0	6.9	1.0
Tajikistan	12.6	5.0	5.0	5.0
Turkmenistan	8.0	1.0	8.0	1.0
Ukraine	0.5	7.0	0	7.0
Uzbekistan	14.7	5.0	12.7	5.0
	29.0	10.0	15.3	10.0

/1. The overall rating consists of a 10-point scale which weighs a country's simple average tariff and the extent of non-tariff barriers. Countries with a scale of 1 to 4 are considered to have broadly open trade regimes. A rating of 5 or 6 indicates moderate trade restrictions. Countries with ratings of 7 to 10 are considered to have restrictive trade regimes.

Source: International Monetary Fund (IMF), (2000; 2003).

As shown in Table 3.1, Kyrgyzstan has one of the lowest import tariffs in the region and import tariffs and duties are not a barrier to trade. However, cross-border customs formalities, customs valuation and inspection process are time consuming and frustrating which act as a tax on international trade.

Kyrgyz Republic has bilateral trade agreements with seven countries. These include the USA (1992), Mongolia (1992), Kazakhstan, Moldova (1996), Russian Federation (1993), Ukraine (1998) and Uzbekistan (1998). It is a member of the Eurasia Economic Community (EURASEC), the Central Asia Economic Union

(CAEU) and Shanghai Co-operation Organization (SCO). It has also gained the membership of the Economic Co-operation Organization (ECO) as well as the UN Special Program for the Economies of Cental Asia (SPECA) and the Central Asia Forum (CAF). It is the first country in Central Asia to join the WTO.

Financial and Banking Sector Reform

In an attempt to open up the economy, Kyrgyzstan adopted the banking law in 1991 and adopted a unified exchange rate regime in 1993. In the same year Kyrgyz introduced its owned currency (som). To reverse the shortage of foreign exchange, the government relaxed restrictions on foreign exchange transactions and introduced a market based exchange rate regime in 1995. In the same year, its currency was made fully convertible for current account transactions. Presently, there are no restrictions in foreign exchange transactions.

Kyrgyzstan has allowed foreign banks to operate in the country since 1992. As a result, the number of foreign banks has increased from one in 1992 to five by the end of 1990s, making the total number of commercial banks 23 in the county by 1999. These banks operate along with domestic commercial banks (1999). There has been a significant fall in the asset share of state-owned banks since the mid 1990s, indicating increasing autonomy in the banking sector. By 1999, the asset share of state-owned banks had fallen to about 21% from 77% in 1994 (Table 3.2). As a part of banking sector reform, domestic credit to loss making banks has been significantly tighten since the mid 1990s. As a result, domestic credit to such enterprises has been reduced to 12.5% of GDP in 1995 to 5.1% by 1999.

Privatization of Public Enterprises

Privatization of public enterprises has proceeded in three stages. Small scale enterprises were privatized in the first stage which was completed by the mid 1990s. In the second stage, medium scale enterprises were privatized, which were completed by late 1990s. Privatization of large scale enterprises is currently under way, but progress has been slow. This is reflected by the lower index of large scale privatization (EBRD index) compared to the index of small scale privatization (Table 3.3). The index for small scale privatization reached 4 as compared to 3 for large scale enterprises by 1999. There has been a significant rise in the share of private sector in GDP, which rose from 15% of GDP in 1991 to 60% by the late 1990s. However, despite growing importance of private sector in the economy, privatization revenue remains very small in Kyrgyzstan. By 1999, revenue from privatization remained below 2% of GDP, despite significant privatization (Table 3.3). This might be due to the fact that in most cases enterprises were sold at much lower prices than the market prices as most privatized enterprises appears to have been bought by employees.

In an attempt to ensure enough liquidity in the economy, the Government has fully liberalized interest rates since the mid 1990s. However, accessing banking sector credit remains a major problem for small and medium enterprises.

Table 3.4 provides information on the number of privatized enterprises during 1993 to 1999. Most of these enterprises are trade and catering (1,916), followed by communal services (1,907) and manufacturing (529).

Although privatization has transferred the ownership structure, these enterprises have not gone through a major restructuring. With the exception of agricultural farms, there have not been any significant improvements in productivity particularly in manufacturing, trade and catering.

Foreign Investment

In an attempt to attract foreign investment Kyrgyzstan has liberalized its policy regime. Foreign investors are also offered several fiscal incentives. For instance, foreign investors enjoy tax holidays between 2 to 5 years depending on the sector they invest in. Export-oriented industries tend to get income tax holidays for a longer period. Foreign firms are also allowed to repatriate 100% of their profit and there are no restrictions as to the foreign share holding. Despite these incentives, foreign investment remains very low and has been highly fluctuating. For example, foreign direct investments (FDI) rose sharply after Kyrgyzstan gained WTO membership and fell since the early 2000. FDI which reached US$96 million in 1995 fell to US$5 million in 2002 and US$17 million in 2003. Among the CIS countries, Kyrgyzstan is the second least popular destination for foreign investment after Tajikistan (per capita foreign investment was less than US$5 in 2001). Tables 3.5 and 3.6 present FDI by activity and their sources.

Table 3.2. Key Indicators of Banking Sector in Kyrgyzstan

	1991	1992	1993	1994	1995	1996	1997	1998	1999
Number of banks (which are foreign owned)	10 (0)	15 (1)	28 (1)	18 (3)	18 (3)	18 (3)	20 (3)	23 (6)	23 (5)
Asset share of state-owned banks (in per cent)	98.8	na	na	77.3	69.7	5.0	8.0	7.1	21.4
Bad loans (in per cent of total loans) [1]	10.0	na	na	92.3	72.0	26.1	7.5	0.2	6.4
Domestic credit to enterprises (in per cent of GDP)	na	na	na	na	12.5	8.7	3.5	5.3	5.1
Stock market capitalization (in per cent of GDP) [2]	na	na	na	na	na	0.3	3.2	23.7	Na
EBRD index of banking sector reform	1.0	1.0	1.0	2.0	2.0	2.0	2.7	2.7	2.3
EBRD index of reform of non-banking financial institutions	1.0	1.0	1.0	1.0	1.7	2.0	2.0	2.0	2.0

Notes:

1. In 1998 all bad loans in the banking system were transferred to a special bank managed by NBKR. The data reported by the central bank are likely to exclude these bad loans.
2. The listing of the state energy company, Kyrgzenergo, accounts for the large increase in capitalization in 1998.

Source: EBRD (2000).

Table 3.3. Key indicators of Privatization in Kyrgyzstan

	1991	1992	1993	1994	1995	1996	1997	1998	1999
Privatization revenues (cumulative, in per cent of GDP)	0.0	0.0	0.2	0.6	0.9	1.3	1.4	1.6	1.9
Private sector share in GDP (in per cent)	15.0	20.0	25.0	30.0	40.0	50.0	60.0	60.0	60.0
EBRD index of small-scale privatization	1.0	2.0	3.0	4.0	4.0	4.0	4.0	4.0	4.0
EBRD index of large-scale privatization	1.0	2.0	2.0	3.0	3.0	3.0	3.0	3.0	3.0

Source: EBRD (2000)

Table 3.4. Kyrgyz Republic: Number of Privatized Units by Economic Sectors

	1993*	1994	1995	1996	1997	1998	1999	Total*
Total	**4428**	**702**	**703**	**327**	**177**	**175**	**146**	**6658**
Manufacturing	259	57	137	23	46	3	4	529
Light manufacturing	42	6	9	1	-	1	1	60
Food manufacturing	77	31	87	4	-	1	1	201
Machinery and metal rolling	56	3	9	1	2	-	-	71
Construction materials	37	5	14	2	2	-	-	60
Others	47	12	18	15	42	1	2	137
Agriculture	235	84	22	10	1	1	3	356
Construction	223	76	74	39	5	15	23	455
Transport	82	21	33	7	14	4	4	165
Communal services	1811	37	19	15	6	16	3	1907
Trade and catering	1626	123	50	87	15	11	4	1916
Supplies	-	12	30	6	59	2	2	111
Public utilities	-	24	31	23	8	36	28	150
Health care, sports and social security	-	174	170	7	-	6	23	380
Education	-	7	2	2	3	7	3	24
Culture and Arts	-	4	6	7	3	7	10	37
Science and scientific research	-	1	-	-	-	-	-	1
Others	192	82	129	101	16	67	39	626

* cumulative

Source: Kyrgyz Republic official website

Table 3.5. FDI in Kyrgyz Republic by Types of Activity (in '000 US$)

	1998	1999	2000	2001	2002	2003
Total	**136301.2**	**108562.1**	**89607.9**	**90088.5**	**115666.1**	**146955.5**
Agriculture, hunting and forestry	299.9	620.3	40.8	130.1	805.3	2009.9
Mining industry	1627.8	4005.1	4607.6	4320.7	5058.2	12285.4
Manufacturing industry	27873.9	55732.4	44026.0	50897.4	52802.4	73164.4
Production and distribution of energy, gas and water	68.5	0.1			31.5	322.6
Construction	21198.6	11647.0	4670.3	129.3	2166.7	5037.7
Trade and repair of motor vehicles, household appliances and articles of personal use	58868.4	15488.5	14686.9	23267.3	19737.8	22626.9
Hotels and restaurants	998.7	130.4	10587.5	6962.6	4812.0	1960.6
Transport and communication	8131.7	794.6	3078.5	2309.2	7954.8	4670.4
Financial activity	5375.3	1663.7	1560.3	469.5	6005.6	3960.5
Real estate operations and rent services	11633.8	18083.4	5600.1	1377.3	13171.7	3544.8
Government management						1393.5
Education	58.7	45.4	72.6	80.1	2612.2	9325.0
Health care and social services	128.6	71.5	0.5	14.9	6.3	5317.6
Housing, social and personal services	37.3	279.7	676.8	130.1	501.6	1336.2

Source: Kyrgyz Republic official website

Table 3.6. Sources of FDI ('000 US$)

	1995	1996	1997	1998	1999	2000	2001	2002	2003
Total	**95926.4**	**153059.5**	**86343.1**	**136301.2**	**108562.1**	**89607.9**	**90088.5**	**115666.1**	**146955.5**
of which:									
outside CIS	**95543.2**	**151732.5**	**84195.0**	**129810.4**	**102757.9**	**76539.3**	**83734.3**	**89551.3**	**119408.7**
Australia	-	-	84.7	269.1	429.4	401.6	79.9	5829.2	201.0
Afghanistan	1.0	137.0	251.8	248.0	33.4	7.6	50.0	31.4	743.3
Bahamas	-	4.0	600.8	48.8	-	60.0	290.0	2.8	-
Great Britain	7.5	577.0	13352.5	20878.9	26121.3	6078.7	1626.6	2542.5	1973.0
Germany	106.3	740.5	1264.4	1940.6	15574.3	9515.1	22401.7	8977.4	5981.8
Israel	164.6	104.0	75.2	97.6	4.2	73.4	44.0	179.6	163.3
India	24.7	49.3	1073.5	2038.2	900.8	1055.7	486.6	695.0	776.2
Indonesia	16.7	88.3	76.9	749.0	168.0	141.5	1507.7	803.2	392.9
Ireland	147.5	782.4	694.6	186.8	44.8	870.6	1.8	51.3	33.7
Italy	10.8	760.4	1942.7	3745.6	3937.7	559.3	0.1	564.7	423.0
Canada	91811.7	126507.7	31402.0	8527.4	4868.3	6756.9	12984.4	12730.0	31121.2
Cyprus	17.8	540.7	72.6	58.5	11.6	753.0	557.8	961.3	1826.3
China	154.6	346.4	274.3	1886.0	1093.5	891.3	2488.1	8538.5	14644.2
Republic of Korea	2.1	-	343.1	13930.3	759.8	61.6	3916.7	7679.4	7217.1
Cuba	165.8	267.1	-	-	0.3	14.5	6.6	-	9.1
Lithuania	0.4	0.3	-	434.8	134.3	5.4	0.4	75.1	173.3
Liechtenstein	-	300.0	-	650.6	-	20.6	-	-	345.0
Malaysia	-	124.0	2505.0	1694.5	90.0	2964.8	188.9	-	-
Netherlands	0.1	365.3	19.4	221.4	30.1	9199.8	1716.4	1116.1	2505.0
United Arab Emirates	-	1.3	15.5	59.6	783.3	583.5	846.1	1138.6	6822.4

Table 3.6. (Continued)

	1995	1996	1997	1998	1999	2000	2001	2002	2003
Total	**95926.4**	**153059.5**	**86343.1**	**136301.2**	**108562.1**	**89607.9**	**90088.5**	**115666.1**	**146955.5**
of which:									
outside CIS	**95543.2**	**151732.5**	**84195.0**	**129810.4**	**102757.9**	**76539.3**	**83734.3**	**89551.3**	**119408.7**
Seychelles	-	-	79.1	262.9	-	-	-	-	-
Pakistan	3.0	19.3	151.1	342.0	167.9	56.3	34.2	43.8	67.7
Poland	-	2.2	19.3	211.1	28.8	10.0	-	210.9	468.4
United States	230.9	4318.2	10007.4	32523.3	19154.3	23577.6	17502.2	20144.1	9881.9
Turkey	559.3	10927.3	17569.2	15436.0	23253.0	12129.8	16334.9	13439.4	25280.6
Switzerland	2004.7	3959.3	1215.9	2962.4	3283.1	429.2	295.4	356.1	3958.6
Japan	4.0	113.0	514.1	9750.7	167.1	14.1	3.6	-	0.1
CIS	**383.2**	**1327.0**	**2148.1**	**6490.8**	**5804.2**	**13068.6**	**6354.2**	**26114.8**	**27546.8**
Azerbaijan	-	-	-	6.6	-	-	3.6	-	-
Armenia	-	0.4	-	-	-	-	-	-	-
Belarus	0.6	3.9	-	20.3	-	479.1	160.0	569.9	1152.3
Georgia	-	3.9	9.2	-	0.6	0.3	-	-	51.0
Kazakhstan	85.3	320.9	1234.0	4434.1	1309.5	210.4	1475	6309.6	13242.4
Republic of Moldova	-	0.2	0.1	-	-	-	-	-	46.1
Russian Federation	263	773.4	688.9	1323.1	1505.2	5426.0	3020.7	17094.7	11125.6
Tajikistan	-	-	4.8	144.9	187.0	275.1	450.4	1645.7	273.4
Turkmenistan	-	5.0	5.3	-	2517.7	6576.3	38.1	-	71.5
Uzbekistan	34.3	190.4	203.1	532.3	222.4	91.4	1206.4	286.4	991.0
Ukraine	-	28.9	2.7	29.5	61.8	10.0	-	208.5	593.5

Source: Kyrgyz Republic official website.

Tajikistan

Trade Policy Regime

Like Kyrgyz Republic, Tajikistan also has very low tariffs and it does not apply non-tariff measures to restrict imports. (Table 3.1). In an attempt to open up its economy, Tajikistan has applied for WTO membership on 29 May 2001. People of Tajikistan believe that the accession to WTO is an important step to create its image in international community as a credible nation for trade and investment. Tajikistan has made significant progress in reducing import tariffs. During 1999 to 2002, import tariffs fell by 60%. In May 2002 import tariffs were unified at 5%, with a few exceptions. According to the IMF, Tajikistan has moderate trade restrictions, scoring 5 out of 10 (Table 3.1).[17] With the introduction of a unified tariff, imports of alcohol and tobacco products, cars, tyres and petroleum products also attract 20% excise duties. All imports are also charged a 20% vale added tax (VAT) and 0.15% customs service fees. There are no other official charges on imports.

While Tajikistan has one of the liberal tariff regimes, time consuming administrative procedures tend to discourage international trade transactions. Also, customs and border formalities significantly discourage import competition and raises cost of exports. At customs, goods are checked manually as there are no automatic machines to scan and weigh the cargo. Pilferage and damage often occur in the loading and unloading process. This significantly increases the cost of international trade transactions.

Unlike Kyrgyz Republic, Tajikistan does not have export restrictions nor does it encourage exports through export processing zones (EPZs). The government claims that its export policy is liberal and it does not see a need for EPZs to promote exports. There are no taxes or charges on exporters, except for a 0.15% customs service fee. All exporters are to be registered at the Ministry of State, Revenues and Duties (MSRD) to be entitled for VAT refunds under the duty drawback scheme. Under Article 58 to 67 of the Customs Code, VAT collected on imported inputs used by exporters are to be refunded once the evidence of exports is presented within two years at the MSRD. Tajikistan does not have export licensing or quota system, however, exporters of narcotics and medical drugs and arms need to obtain permission from the government. While these export policies appear to be liberal, exporters have to spend a significant amount of time in

[17] The overall rating consists of a 10-point scale, which weighs a country's simple average tariff and the extent of non-tariff barriers. Countries with a scale of 1 to 4 are considered to have broadly open trade regimes. A rating of 5 or 6 indicates moderate trade restrictions. Countries with ratings of 7 to 10 are considered to have restrictive trade regimes.

obtaining official documents for meeting customs formalities. For instance, exporters are required to obtain a Certificate of Consistency (from the Tajikstandart) to ensure that goods meet export standard and a Certificate of Origin has also to be obtained from the Chamber of Commerce. Also, they are required to submit export contract, export license (in the case of items requiring a licensing) and the Deal Certificate issued by a commercial bank to the border customs office. In addition to the above formalities involved in obtaining official documents, both exporters and importers face substantial delays in the cross-border formalities because goods are checked manually and shippers are required to fill in several forms at the entry and exit customs points.

Due to its land-locked position, any thing imported into or exported from Tajikistan by road or rail has to pass through Uzbekistan, Kazakhstan and Tukmenistan.[18] Currently, Tajikistan's cargo passing through Uzbekistan requires to make an official deposit equal to 100% of the value of the consignment in US$ which, in principle, is refunded as soon as the cargo leaves the Uzbek's border.[19] However, Tajik businessmen claim that there are problems in getting the deposit back and often it is not paid in US dollars but in local currency. Since 2002 Uzbekistan has introduced a new restriction under which 82 Tajik export commodities including mineral fertilizers, aluminium and chemical products require prior approval from the Uzbek government even to use its territories for exporting to third countries. The Uzbek government charges a service fee of 0.5% of the value of the consignment. The Uzbek government claims that tight restrictions are exercised to prevent smuggling of imported goods and illegal drugs. Smuggling occurs due to differentiate tariffs between the countries.[20] This is against the GATT Article V which outlines Freedom of Transit (Appendix III). Transit problems have significantly hindered trade and industrial development in Tajikistan. Like traders in Kyrgyz Republic, their counterparts in Tajikistan also face severe transit problems when goods are transported by road due to transit

[18] Tajikistan's exports to and imports from Europe are done by railways through Iliychevsk port in Ukraine, which is about 5,000 km from Dushanbe. Any thing it exports or imports has to go through Uzbekistan, Kazakhstan, Turkemnistan and Russia.

[19] If a deposit is not paid, then a Customs Officer will accompany the cargo up to the exit border. An official fee is charged for this service.

[20] Nepal's experience is worth discussing here. Being a land-locked country, Nepal faced similar problems like many CIS countries until the early 1990s because its trade regime was more liberal than that of India. This created an incentive for re-exporting of imported foreign goods from Nepal to India. To prevent this, India exercised tight cross-border formalities, which hurt genuine exporters and importers. Following the opening up of the Indian economy in 1991 and harmonization of trade taxes between India and Nepal, the incentive for smuggling from Nepal to India vanished. Harmonization in trade policy between the countries reduced cross-border

permit, visa and other requirements. This significantly adds the cost of exports and imports.

Republic of Tajikistan has trade relations with 80 countries. As of 2003, it has signed bilateral trade agreements with 28 countries, which include all CIS countries, except Georgia and 17 non-CIS countries. The non-CIS countries with whom it has the bilateral trade agreements are USA, Austria, Bulgaria, Hungary, Vietnam, India, China, Pakistan, Slovakia, Turkey, Czech Republic, Romania, Yugoslavia, Kuwait, Iran, Afghanistan and Syria. Under the bilateral trade agreements preferential access is granted to each other's market on most favoured nation (MFN) basis. While Tajikistan has preferential access to European and American markets for its exports of manufactured goods and agricultural products under the generalized system of preferences (GSP), she has not been able to fully utilize this privilege due to the weak infrastructure and the poor production base.

Tajikistan is a member of EURASEC, which includes Belarus, Kyrgyz Republic, Kazakhstan and the Russian Federation. It was created in 2000 to promote trade and economic cooperation among the members within the framework of customs union. From the beginning it had agreed to remove all tariffs and non-tariff barriers among the members and keep external tariffs lower. However, very little progress has been made so far. EURASEC aims to have a common external tariff by 2010. Since 1999 it has joined Central Asia Economic Union (CAEU), which was formed by Kazakhstan, Kyrgyzstan and Uzbekistan in 1995. It aims to promote trade among members by removing barriers. In reality, however, it has not happened as Uzbekistan is reluctant to liberalize its trade regime and Tajikistan faces several problems in Transit in Uzbekistan. Tajikistan is also a member of the Shanghai Cooperative Organization (SCO), which includes Kazakhstan, Kyrgyz Republic, Uzbekistan, Russia and China. It was established to promote free trade and maintain security in the region. As yet, no progress has been made in these directions. Tajikistan can gain considerably from SCO once the rehabilitation of Silk Road is completed which will give a direct access to Chinese markets. Republic of Tajikistan is also a member of ECO, SPECA and CAF.

Banking Sector Reform

Following independence, several commercial banks were established by the State to support the transition to a market economy. As a result the number of commercial banks rose from one in the 1980s to 18 by the mid 1990's. However,

formalities, customs clearance time and improved bilateral relations. (Further discussion can be found in Sharma 1999.)

they suffer from bad loans (higher non-performing loans) due to excessive government interventions. By 1999, shares of bad loans in total loans reached about 16% Table 3.7). Higher non-performing loans have significantly limited the lending ability of the banking sector and made its lending policy highly security-driven. This has made access to banking sector loans difficult for small and medium scale enterprises (SMEs) and poverty driven farmers. Also, loans are granted only if 150% collateral security is provided which is extremely difficult for SMEs. Although significant reforms have taken place since the mid 1990s, including deregulation of interest rates and permission for foreign commercial banks to operate in the country, the sector still suffers from inefficiency. For example, commercial banks reliance on domestic debt is high and rising. By the end of 1990s credit absorbed by these enterprises were equal to 10% of GDP (Table 3.7).

Currently, there are 20 commercial banks in the country, of which three are foreign banks. Apart from traditional banking functions, these commercial banks also perform functions such as opening the letter of credits (LCs) and transferring money from Tajikistan to other countries by telegraphic transfer and/or bank cheques. Depending on the nature of services, banking fees vary from 0.5 to 2% of the transactions. Agroinvestbank has even introduced a credit card which is accepted world-wide, although inside the country it is hardly accepted, as local businesses, including big hotels, do not know how to use it nor do they have the facility to use it.

The banking sector has yet to be fully develop in Tajikistan. The business community feels that there are too many fees and charges in the banking system. As a result, most SMEs keep their liquidity in US dollars and at home rather than in the banking system. This has also limited the banking sector's lending ability. Recently three finance companies have emerged in the private sector. However, their services are available only to shareholders. As these finance companies grow, they may be able to extend their services to non-members. This is definitely a move to make the state dominated banking system more competitive. National Bank of Tajikistan, with the help of ADB, is developing the Micro Finance Institutions (MFIs) in various parts of the country, which will significantly improve the access to finance for SMEs.

Table 3.7. Key Indicators of the Banking Sector in Tajikistan

	1991	1992	1993	1994	1995	1996	1997	1998	1999
Number of banks (of which foreign owned)	10.0 (na)	10.0 (na)	15.0 (na)	17.0 (na)	18.0 (na)	23.0 (na)	28.0 (5.0)	20.0 (5.0)	20.0 (3.0)
Asset share of state-owned banks (in per cent)	na	na	na	na	na	5.3	30.3	29.2	6.9
Bad loans (in per cent of total loans)	na	na	na	na	na	2.9	3.0	3.2	15.8
Domestic credit to enterprises (in per cent of GDP) [1]	na	na	na	na	na	4.0	4.8	7.7	10.0
Stock market capitalization (in per cent of GDP)	na	na	na	na	na	na	Na	na	Na
EBRD index of banking sector reform	1.0	1.0	1.0	1.0	1.0	1.0	1.0	1.0	1.0
EBRD index of reform of non-banking financial institutions	1.0	1.0	1.0	1.0	1.0	1.0	1.0	1.0	1.0

Note: 1. Data from IMF. Excludes special cotton financing from NBT.
Source: EBRD (2002).

Foreign Exchange Regime

Tajikistan had a tight exchange control regime until the end of 1999. Apart from the foreign exchange surrender requirements, the government introduced the foreign exchange duty on remittances in 1992. The foreign exchange surrender requirements acted as a tax on exporters because they had to sell their foreign exchange earnings at lower rates, which prompted under-invoicing of exports, while the foreign exchange duty encouraged unofficial inflows of foreign exchange. Both undermined the future of the banking system. In 1996, the government abolished the foreign exchange surrender requirements and adopted a unified exchange rate regime. In the same year the local currency was made fully convertible to all current account transactions. In early 2000, the foreign exchange duty was abolished. Currently, there are no restrictions in foreign exchange transactions. Although, local somoni is fully convertible, traders tend to keep their earnings in the American dollar.

Privatization of Public Enterprises

With the implementation of privatization program in the mid 1990's, the private sector share in GDP has increased gradually. Its share doubled within four years, from 15% of GDP in 1995 to 30% 1999. Similarly, revenue generated through the privatization increased from less than 2% of GDP to 4% in the same period (Table 3.8). Privatization program has encouraged the private sector's participation in small business and trading activities.

In an attempt to deregulate agricultural market, monopoly of state trading corporations in the importation and distribution of agricultural input was abolished and the licensing requirement for agriculture trade was eliminated in the mid 1990s. Deregulation of agriculture input and output markets, together with the privatization of land and the deregulation of grain and bread prices, significantly boost up agricultural production, particularly wheat and cotton production, leading to an increase in exports. However, public sector still has a significant control in aluminium production, production and distribution of electricity, railways and road transport. Buses and trucks have been privatized, and their services have considerably improved, particularly the services of urban transportation. Most small enterprises were privatized by 2000 and over 50% of large enterprises have been privatized by 2002.

Table 3.8. Key Indicators of Privatization in Tajikistan

	1991	1992	1993	1994	1995	1996	1997	1998	1999
Share of small firms privatized (%)1	0.4	10.5	11.4	15.8	20.9	29.9	39.7	56.9	75.3
Private revenue (cumulative, in per cent of GDP)	0.0	0.7	0.9	1.1	1.5	1.6	2.1	2.8	4.0
Private sector share in GDP (in per cent)	10.0	10.0	10.0	15.0	15.0	20.0	20.0	30.0	30.0
EBRD index of small-scale privatization	1.0	2.0	2.0	2.0	2.0	2.0	2.3	3.0	3.0
EBRD index of large-scale privatization	1.0	1.0	1.0	1.0	2.0	2.0	2.0	2.0	2.3

Note: 1 data from State property Committee. According to the IMF, out of 6000 firms eligible around 5,500 were privatized by the mid 2000.

Source: EBRD (2000).

There has been, however, slow progress in privatizing electricity generation and distribution, road and railways which are essential for trade and industrial development. By early 2003, about 50% of manufacturing industries have been privatized. Despite this, production and exports of manufactured goods, textiles and garments in particular, have not increased. Most of these manufacturing industries were established during the Soviet regime and they need to be modernized, but due to the lack of finance, it has not been done. Also, poor business climate remains a major problem in the private sector development in Tajikistan as well as in other Central Asian countries (Appendix IV). Brunetti *et al.* (2001) in a rating of 1 (lowest obstacles) to 22 (highest obstacles) found that the Central Asian countries scored 19, indicating the poor state of business climate for the private sector development.

Foreign Investment

Despite opening up the economy, Tajikistan is the least popular destination for foreign investors among the CIS countries mainly due to the lack of appropriate business climate. Business climate is poor because of the inefficient institutions, infrastructure and red tape. Per capita foreign investment remains very low (less than US$2) and has not significantly increased until now. Foreign Investment Law offers several incentives as well as guarantees that such investment will not be nationalized. The Law allows foreign investors to purchase land and mines. Also, there are no restrictions as to the share of foreign holdings, and foreign investment is allowed in most sectors. Foreign investors are permitted to repatriate 100% of profits. Foreign investment in the form of intellectual property is protected by the Law (Article 26 of the Foreign Investment Law).Tax holidays for foreign investment is one of the important provisions of the Foreign Investment Law (Article 18) which vary from 2 to 5 years, depending on the amount of investment. For example, foreign investment between US$100,000 to US$500,000 is exempt from profit tax for 2 years, while foreign investment of over US$5 million is exempt from tax for 5 years. It appears that by offering tax concessions on the basis of capital investment, foreign investment policy has encouraged capital intensive rather than labour-intensive investment. Despite these reforms Tajikistan has not been able to attract a large number of investments due to weak enforcement of law and order, poor infrastructure, and transit and customs related problems. It is in this context, Tajikistan's integration to the rest of the world through the membership of WTO is important. Gaining WTO membership is important for Tajikistan for several reasons (Drabek and Laird, 1997 and Michaloboulos, 1998). Firstly, WTO membership improves domestic institutions and policies, leading to an improvement in Tajikistan's image as a credible nation for trade and investment. Secondly, WTO membership improves market access because about 90% of the world market exists among the WTO members. Being a member, Tajikistan will have unconditional market access on MFN basis. Thirdly, membership of WTO provides access to a powerful dispute settlement mechanism, which is otherwise difficult to access. Fourthly, it sends clear signals to potential investors and international financial institutions that the country is committed to liberalize. Since international financial institutions tide their loans with the level of liberalization, joining WTO, or even applying for its membership, can attract much needed development assistance.

CONCLUSION

Both Kyrgyz Republic and Tajikistan have very low tariffs and they do not apply non-tariff measures to restrict imports. Both have a liberal exchange rate regime and meet IMF Article VIII standards. There are no restrictions on currency exchange. They are also the members of several regional organizations which are created to promote economic cooperation. Kyrgyzstan was the first country in region to obtain WTO membership, while Tajikistan applied for its membership on 29 May 2001, which is an important step to create its image as a credible nation. However, Tajikistan accession to WTO depends on several factors. These included development of market-based institutions, appropriate legal environment and simplication of cross-border formalities. The development of these will require both financial and technical resources, which Tajikistan lacks. International community can provide valuable help in this respect.

Chapter 4

TRADE IN TRANSITIONAL ECONOMIES: KYRGYZ REPUBLIC AND TAJIKISTAN

INTRODUCTION

The purpose of this chapter is to analyse the performance of foreign trade in Kyrgyz Republic and Tajikistan. It should be kept in mind that the official trade statistics do not reflect the actual trade volumes because of the prevalence of smuggling and the under-reporting of trade transactions. The actual volume of trade could be as high as 20% of the official figures. The chapter is organized as follow. First, Kyrgyz Republic trade performance is examined followed by the assessment of trade performance of Tajikistan.

ASSESSMENT OF TRADE PERFORMANCE OF KYRGYZ REPUBLIC

Kyrgyz Republic's exports almost doubled during the 1993 to 1997 period. It grew from US$334 million in 1993 to about US$604 million in 1997. However, export growth was not sustained after 1998 mainly due to the Russian Financial crisis of August 1997, as Russia and other FSU countries were the major destinations of its exports. The share of exports in GDP fell from about 39% in 1993 to 31% by 2001. Even by 2003, the share of exports in GDP remained less than 40%. The 1997 Russian Financial crisis also had an impact on import front. Imports dropped from US$709 million in 1997 to US$587 million by 2002, although some recovered was made in 2003 (Table 4.1). The share of imports in

GDP fell from 51% in 1998 to about 42% by 2003. Since import growth has been higher than growth in exports, trade deficit remains very high, although it declined somewhat in the early 2000 (Figure 4.1). In 2003 Kyrgyzstan terms of trade improved marginally compared to the previous year. However, in comparison to the base year (1995=100), its terms of trade deteriorated by 6 % in 2002 and 5% in 2003 mainly due to higher prices of its imports in comparison to exports. Table 4.1 presents performance of foreign trade sector in Kyrgyz Republic.

Figure 4.1 shows trends in exports, imports and trade balance during 1992 to 2003. Kyrgyzstan's imports are growing more rapidly than exports, leading to a persistent trade deficit since the mid 1990s, although the growing deficit was somewhat arrested in the early 2000.

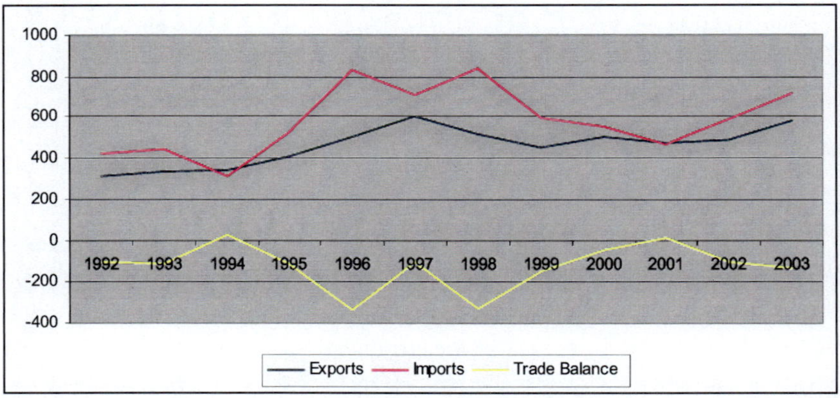

Source: ADB (2002a and 2004).

Figure 4.1.Trends in Exports, Imports and Trade Deficit in Kyrgyzstan (in million US$)

The composition of Kyrgyzstan's exports is presented in Table 4.2. Kyrgyzstan has experienced a significant fluctuation in its exports. The share of agriculture in total export earnings has fallen from 10% in the mid 1990s to about 3% by 2002. Not only the share of agriculture has fallen but also the absolute value to agricultural exports has declined (see Table 4.2). Since Kyrgyzstan's economy mainly relies on agriculture which contributes over 50% to GDP and employs a large number of workforce, this decline in agricultural exports appears to have increased economic hardship, particularly in rural areas. The share of manufacturing products in total exports remains very low, although its share has increased from 2% in 1995 to about 6% by 2002. Within manufacturing, exports of lamps and car parts and equipments have increased rapidly. Exports of coal and electricity have been widely fluctuating mainly due to inefficiency of state-owned electricity authority. In fact, production and exports of electricity have been fluctuating and the country still imports electricity despite enormous potential in hydro-electricity generation. However, exports of kerosene have increased rapidly, from US$1.7 thousands in 1995 to US$34.9 million in 2002. Although Kyrgyzstan has tremendous potential in exports of textile and footwear, their exports remain very low. Textile and garments together contributed about 10% to the country's export earning by 2002.

The composition of Kyrgyzstan's imports is reported in Table 4.3. Its imports consist of a large number of manufactured goods, contributing about 12% to total imports in 2002. The share of energy imports is about 24% in total imports of the country. Despite huge potential in electricity production and exports, its reliance on imports of electricity and gas has been increasing. Although imports of agricultural products have been declining, about 5% of total imports are dominated by such products, including wheat, flour, vegetable oils and sugar cane.

Tables 4.4 and 4.5 present direction of Kyrgyzstan's exports and imports. In both exports and imports, shares of Russia and the FSU countries of Central Asia have fallen, while that of Asian and European countries have increased. Kyrgyzstan's exports to and imports from America, Australia and Oceania, and Africa remain very small (just over 2% share in total exports).

Europe is a major destination for Kyrgyzstan's exports (54%) followed by Russia and the FSU countries of the Central Asia (34%) and Asia (11%). Europe has emerged as a popular destination for Kyrgyzstan's exports as reflected by the rising share of its exports to these countries. The share of Europe in Kyrgyzstan's exports rose from 37% in 1997 to 54% by 2001. Although the share of Russia and the FSU countries of Cental Asia as a group has fallen from 50% in 1997 to 34% share by 2001, it is the second popular destination for Kyrgyzstan's exports.

Even after disintegration from the FSU Russia remains a major trading partner for Kyrgyzstan's exports, although its share has fallen from 16% in 1997 to 14% by 2001. Among the FSU countries of Cental Asia, Uzbekistan remains a major market for its exports, but its share has been fluctuating from 17% in 1997 to 10% by 2001. Protectionist sentiment in Uzbekistan and deteriorating bilateral relations appear to have contributed to a fall in Kyrgyzstan's exports to and imports from Uzbekistan. Kyrgyzstan's exports to Kazakhstan have significantly fallen in recent years. For example, the share of latter's in the former's total exports fell from 14% in 1997 to 8% by 2001. The shares of other countries in the region remain very small. Table 4.4 presents the direction of Kyrgyzstan's exports.

Table 4.1. Kyrgyz Public: Performance of Foreign Trade

	1993	1995	1997	1998	1999	2000	2001	2002	2003
Merchandise Exports (Million US$)	339.6	408.9	603.8	513.6	453.8	504.5	476.1	485.5	536.5
Merchandise Imports (Million US$)	447.8	522.3	709.3	841.5	599.7	554.1	467.2	587.2	908.2
Export Price Index (1995=100)	56	-	-	-	-	-	-	100	115
Import Price Index (1995=100)	53	-	-	-	-	-	-	107	121
Terms of Trade (1995=100)	105							94	95
Trade deficit % GDP	12.4	7.6	6.0	19.9	11.7	3.6	0.6	6.7	7.8
Exports % of GDP	38.9	27.4	34.1	31.3	36.3	36.8	31.2	39.6a	38.0a
Imports % of GDP	51.3	35.0	40.1	51.3	48.0	40.4	30.6	43.3a	42.2a

Note: a Also includes exports of services
Source: ADB (2002a and 2004) Export and import price indices and terms of trade data come from the World Bank website.

Table 4.2. Kyrgyz Republic: Exports of Major Commodities in Thousand US$

	1995	1996	1997	1998	1999	2000	2001	2002
Total	**408938.476**	**505396.6**	**603807.86**	**513635.84**	**453835.6**	**504489.18**	**476151.63**	**485544.02**
including:								
Vegetables	12592.314	12456.735	9807.891	9222.45	5108.1			
Fruits	7125.449	8095.373	6390.47	2573.85	3242.9			
Vegetables and fruits	19717.763	20552.108	16198.361	14668.86	10154.968	9118.096	10936.532	16248.418
Wheat	6.249	3521.011	1259.44	2469.91	233.2	126.235	676.831	174.226
Flour	733.716	4367.267	7386.81	4830.54	4521.1	3226.534	307.72	373.22
Sugar	15365.696	52058.396	17737.239	7956.756	3736.8	921.534	1863.628	5253.14
Wax	3049.398	4118.087	4721.167	2276.69	1538.4	958.607	672.996	471.674
Tobacco	21644.358	16265.545	31683.18	49236.13	42076	30154.476	25390.621	19710.634
Cigarettes	166.8	1795.052	1374.97	1836.9	999.1	1133.595	883.169	61.995
Cement	2066.596	6031.866	9995.35	9868.15	1084.2	1983.07	1539.98	1541.671
Coal	3138.415	2028.001	1774.65	481.63	212.5	161.465	178.686	707.584
Kerosene	1.7	1.245	-	1311.076	1179.705	1561.36	5764.906	34960.163
Electricity	40967.781	73550.493	83218.018	25581.036	52042.3	79782.7	46821.85	22039.826
Products of inorganic chemistry	20356.93	32209.22	11672.68	12779.07	12632.2	12721.288	16273.22	23641.426
Skins of cattle	2131.233	10818.16	7941.49	3804.9	1474.1	4721.016	6084.734	17165.22
Skins of sheep	1819.86	4235.412	2465.72	2173.15	1099.9	1970.288	2334.252	1955.628
Wool	19173.581	4825.998	3177.93	1313.393	1089.4	2117.05	1421.79	2395.981
Wool yarn	4042.943	1965.535	2844.68	2613.21	800.1	45.995	136.429	386.866
Woollen fabrics	2798.573	2216.613	1348.04	1217.54	375.9	306.113	363.564	292.636

Table 4.2. (Continued)

	1995	1996	1997	1998	1999	2000	2001	2002
Total	**408938.476**	**505396.6**	**603807.86**	**513635.84**	**453835.6**	**504489.18**	**476151.63**	**485544.02**
including:								
Yarn	23662.138	32856.436	27801.81	20969.63	21111.5	32344.916	22115.732	45171.67
Cotton fabrics	6268.714	4641.836	3900.2	2257.46	1827.3	1238.736	306.919	498.963
Stale	1729.337	3077.06	4264.17	5226.55	3618.4	2981.84	4280.941	5601.368
Mirrors	4173.708	7363.94	4932.826	3688.15	758.9	172.934	21.4	2295.058
Metal scrap (copper)	11775.15	8668.123	10197.404	4415.22	3972.9	5295.877	904.592	1457.006
Metal scrap (aluminium)	3983.023	1508.361	3300.84	3948.49	14722.5	19337.281	1933.012	4285.988
Lamps	10067.482	14107.893	14665.994	13314.35	9637.2	11590.064	12266.134	13795.225
Car parts and equipment	4359.063	3963.745	4850.56	7538.4	7007.3	2202.733	3995.123	7316.988
Not classified	-	2.3	184339.4	195819.37	183117.8	195347.88	224573.3	162758.88
% Share in Total Exports of								
Agriculture	10.5	10.7	7.4	5.4	5.7	2.3	2.5	3.5
Manufacturing	2.2	13.9	8.4	7.9	5.2	5.3	3.9	5.7
Energy	11.1	15.1	14.0	5.3	11.6	16.1	11.1	12.1
Textile and Clothing	14.0	9.2	6.5	5.1	5.5	7.1	5.1	10

Note: The classifications of exports of agriculture, manufacturing, energy, and textile and clothing are based as follows: Agricultural exports include vegetable and fruits. Manufacturing includes sugar, cigarettes, cement, lamps and car parts and equipments while energy includes coal, electricity and kerosene. Textile and clothing includes wool, wool yarn, woollen fabrics, yarn and cotton fabrics.

Source: Kyrgyz Republic official website

Table 4.3. Kyrgyz Republic: Imports of Major Commodities in Thousand US$

	1995	1996	1997	1998	1999	2000	2001	2002
Total	**522334.9**	**837688.2**	**709304.9**	**841504.1**	**599739.8**	**554113.7**	**467242.1**	**586752.5**
including:								
Tea	793.3	1548.6	4683.8	8354.4	5660.9	5241.8	5195.1	2124.4
Wheat	12447.6	22303.8	25549.1	8583.8	15501.9	33271.9	6673.5	11749.2
Flour	10540.9	11592.4	1829.9	2069.8	1784.7	418.0	277.9	3923.0
Vegetable oils	5143.0	4449.2	9796.6	12840.1	5581.6	2955.2	2933.1	3491.2
Sugar-cane	25789.7	83661.8	20482.6	28490.2	6351.3	-	1482.5	3280.0
Sugar	3225.4	2705.8	2344.4	822.9	4861.5	2897.5	4526.8	8679.2
Beer	2843.5	3199.5	1983.8	3429.3	1318.2	2843.9	3940.3	5495.4
Cigarettes	889.4	2330.1	3932.9	4385.3	8365.5	11022.8	9783.1	7805.3
Asbestos	2016.7	2417.4	3058.6	2791.5	2831.0	1936.2	1930.1	2538.0
Coal	17000.9	25143.4	7014.5	17467.5	19592.5	11106.3	6386.9	13926.4
Crude oil	474.9	1230.8	10912.3	7372.1	4235.0	2768.3	-	848.6
Petrol	52525.4	43698.6	34575.4	60456.8	28840.5	24019.9	22136.8	20794.2
Kerosene	11144.6	15625.6	9792.6	13730.3	7712.1	11508.4	11817.4	42504.8
Diesel	22172.9	21477.7	17889.9	12138.2	12988.0	17196.2	19930.1	11796.7
Heavy oils	7805.2	13337.9	3344.0	6015.8	2005.0	4113.2	1223.9	1063.0
Natural gas	55510.7	71795.8	69650.4	72552.9	33026.9	33233.8	33160.4	41760.7
Electricity	8579.0	26717.9	23836.8	7907.1	2840.6	7568.7	9843.1	9738.0
Organic chemical combinations	1534.9	1633.5	6124.1	18838.7	4465.9	4577.6	2996.4	4522.4
Medicines	7680.1	15872.1	17856.9	18233.2	15903.7	20358.2	20545.3	26668.7
Fertilizers	3744.6	10742.2	6463.5	5757.5	1558.2	2761.9	1936.8	2644.9

Table 4.3. (Continued)

	1995	1996	1997	1998	1999	2000	2001	2002
Total	**522334.9**	**837688.2**	**709304.9**	**841504.1**	**599739.8**	**554113.7**	**467242.1**	**586752.5**
including:								
Tyres	3983.3	7099.5	7514.3	9869.6	5987.3	8750.0	6934.9	9927.4
Paper	5427.6	9313.7	11933.6	15194.4	9055.3	11704.5	10846.5	10662.3
Publications	930.9	1663.2	3516.3	16568.7	3229.4	4037.2	1972.7	1823.4
Footwear	2668.9	1987.6	6848.0	10380.3	4579.6	3979.7	3495.2	5003.0
Parts of cars	10272.0	22194.7	10050.8	4572.2	8703.0	10241.3	5579.6	2449.6
Not classified	4139.1	2019.5	21158.8	24581.0	13756.7	11014.7	10071.9	17523.7
% Share in Total Imports of								
Agriculture	10.4	24.5	8.7	6.7	5.7	7.4	3.2	5.1
Manufacturing	5.3	6.1	7.1	9.7	7.8	10.9	12.7	12.3
Energy	33.5	24.7	28.3	23.2	18.2	20.2	22.1	23.9
Footwear	0.5	0.2	1.0	1.2	0.7	0.7	0.6	0.8

Note: Agricultural products include tea, wheat, flour, vegetable oils and sugar-cane. Manufacturing includes sugar, beer, cigarettes, medicines, fertilizers, tyres and paper. Energy includes coal, crude oil, petrol, kerosene, diesel, heavy oils, natural gas, electricity.

Source: Kyrgyz Republic official website.

Table 4.4. Kyrgyz Republic: Direction of Exports (Thousand US$)

Destination	1997	1998	1999	2000	2001
Europe	223708.1 (37.0)	248828.4 (48.0)	215987.1 (48.0)	227522.2 (45.0)	257817.9 (54.0)
Asia	59256.6 (10.0)	39835.3 (8.0)	51275.3 (11.0)	73882.1 (15.0)	50115.7 (11.0)
America	18030.8 (3.0)	7689.6 (1.0)	11624.2 (3.0)	2937.3 (1.0)	8339.8 (2.0)
Africa	6.8 (0.0)	19.7 (0.0)	453.6 (0.0)	1983.8 (0.0)	39.1 (0.0)
Australia and Oceania	121.7 (0.0)	4.8 (0.0)	1.8 (0.0)	12.8 (0.0)	9.6 (0.0)
Russia and FSU countries of Cental Asia	302683.9 (50.0)	217258.1 (42.0)	174493.6 (38.0)	198151 (39.0)	159829.6 (34.0)
Russia	98844.9 (16.0)	83679.3 (16.0)	70713.1 (16.0)	65125.1 (13.0)	64510.2 (14.0)
Kazakhstan	87094 (14.0)	85516.4 (17.0)	44960.1 (10.0)	33393.8 (7.0)	39032.2 (8.0)
Tajikistan	12666.3 (2.0)	8299.2 (2.0)	9463 (2.0)	7489.2 (1.0)	6743.3 (1.0)
Turkmenistan	2566.5 (0.0)	1220.8 (0.0)	(2788.7) (1.0)	(2729.3) (1.0)	(1546.3) (0.0)
Uzbekistan	101512.2 (17.0)	38542.4 (0.08)	46568.7 (10.0)	89413.6 (18.0)	47997.6 (10.0)
Total	**603807.9**	**513635.9**	**453835.6**	**504489.2**	**476151.7**

Note: Figures in parentheses are percentage shares.
Source: Kyrgyz Republic official website.

Table 4.5. Kyrgyz Republic: Direction of Imports (Thousand US$)

Destination	**1997**	**1998**	**1999**	**2000**	**2001**
Europe	125855.7 (18.0)	170989 (20.0)	137359.4 (23.0)	93503.5 (17.0)	79368.2 (17.0)
Asia	123622.3 (17.0)	167573.9 (20.0)	131722.3 (22.0)	109261.7 (20.0)	101744.5 (22.0)
America	44884.8 (6.0)	81789.6 (10.0)	85235.5 (14.0)	65631.7 (12.0)	41437.3 (9.0)
Africa	150.2 (0.0)	3271.4 (0.0)	1483.6 (0.0)	89.9 (0.0)	275.5 (0.0)
Australia and Oceania	322.2 (0.0)	1692.4 (0.0)	102.6 (0.0)	467.9 (0.0)	350.9 (0.0)
Russia and FSU Countries of Central Asia	414469.7 (58.0)	416187.8 (49.0)	243836.4 (41.0)	285160.9 (51.0)	244065.7 (52.0)
Russia	190799.2 (27.0)	204057.8 (24.0)	109366.1 (18.0)	132614.6 (24.0)	85052.1 (18.0)
Kazakhstan	69602.8 (10.0)	75297.7 (9.0)	72679.9 (12.0)	57399.7 (10.0)	81801.4 (18.0)
Tajikistan	9992.3 (1.0)	6375.8 (1.0)	4041.3 (1.0)	1908.9 (0.0)	1501.5 (0.0)
Turkmenistan	15463.4 (2.0)	8214.5 (1.0)	7780.6 (1.0)	18664.6 (3.0)	8977.3 (2.0)
Uzbekistan	128612 (18.0)	122242 (15.0)	49968.5 (8.0)	74573.1 (13.0)	66733.4 (14.0)
Total	**709304.9**	**841504.1**	**599739.8**	**554113.7**	**467242.1**

Note: Figures in parentheses are percentage shares

Source: Kyrgyz Republic official website

About 50% of Kyrgyzstan's imports originate from Russia and the FSU countries of Central Asia, although its share has fallen since 1998 from 58% in 1997 to 52% in 2001 (Table 4.5). Among this group of countries, Russia and Kazakhstan are the major suppliers, each accounting for 18% share in Kyrgyzstan's total imports in 2001. During 1997-2001, Russia's share fell from 27% to 18%, while that of Kazakhstan rose from 10% to 18%. Uzbekistan's share in Kyrgyzstan's total imports fell from 18% in 1997 to 14% by 2001. Other Central Asian countries are marginal players in Kyrgyzstan's imports. Table 4.5 presents the direction of imports.

As stated earlier Kyrgyz Republic has a huge potential in hydro-electricity. Despite this, it has not been able to increase its production and exports which appear to be mainly due to the inefficiency of the State Agency for Energy (SAE). Kyrgyzstan has potential in production and exports of vegetables due to the climatic conditions. However, exports of these commodities require just-in-time delivery. The provision of efficient transport facility and minimum border and customs formalities can significantly increase Kyrgyzstan's exports of vegetables to regional markets. Since these activities are labour intensive, they will help create employment opportunities. Kyrgyz Republic has abundant supplies of pearls, precious and semi-precious stones and gold. Currently, these precious stones and metals are not processed into jewelleries, which could attract higher prices in international markets. Kyrgyzstan's export potential has not yet been fully exploited mainly due to the internal and regional factors rather than the external factors. These factors include the poor institutions and physical infrastructure, tight border and customs formalities, and excessive regulations.

Assessment of Trade Performance of Tajikistan

Like Kyrgyz Republic, Tajikistan has also experienced a decline in both exports and imports after the 1997 Russian Financial crisis. However, its exports and imports picked up from the early 2000 as shown in Figure 4.2. Rising trade deficit remains a major problem in Tajikistan.

It should be noted that despite fluctuations in exports, strong commodity prices contributed to an improvement in Tajikistan's terms of trade during 1993 to 2002 (except for 1997, see Table 4.6). During the period under review, Tajikistan received higher prices for its exports than what it paid for imports (except for 1997). During the 1993 to 2002 period, taking 1993 as a base year, unit value of Tajikistan's exports increased by 43%, while that of imports increased by 4%, contributing to an improvement in terms of trade by 38%. An improvement in terms of trade helped improve the current account deficit from 18% of GDP in 1992 to about 8% by 2001. Table 4.6 presents the performance of Tajikistan's foreign trade.

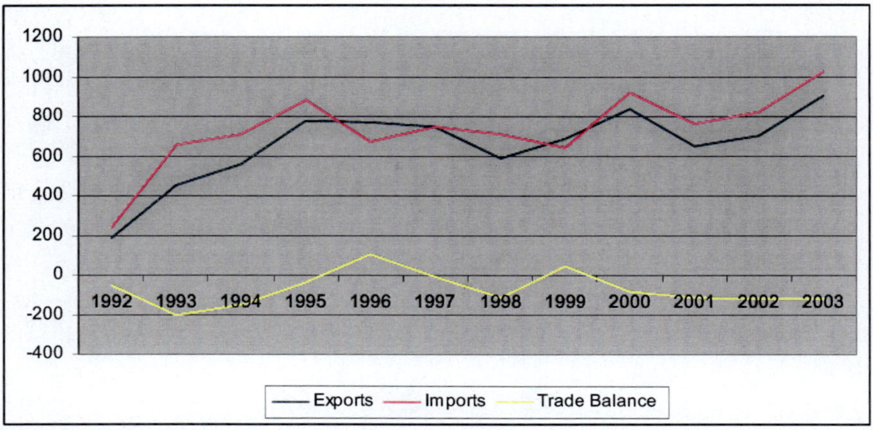

Sources: ADB (2002a and 2004).

Figure 4.2. Trends in Tajikistan's Exports, Imports and Trade Balance (in million US$)

Figures 4.3, 4.4 and 4.5 presents direction of Tajikistan's foreign trade in 2003. As shown in Figure 4.3, Russia and FSU countries are Tajikistan's major trading partners. About 45% of Tajikistan's imports originate from Russia and FSU countries. EU supplies about 9% and Asian countries of Tajik imports about 6% (Figure 4.4). The major destinations for Tajikistan exports are European countries which absorb about 40% of Tajikistan's exports, while Asian countries absorb 31%, and Russia and FSU countries 20% (Figure 4.5).

While Russia and the FSU countries of Central Asia, as a group, remain major destinations for its exports, its exports to the FSU countries of Central Asia have dramatically fallen, particularly to Kazakhstan. In recent years Tajikistan has been successful in penetrating into other markets particularly in Asia. With regard to imports, Russia and the FSU countries of Central Asia, as a group, remain major sources of Tajikistan's imports and contributed about 45% to Tajikistan's total imports by 2003. Table 4.7 presents the magnitude of FDI in Tajikistan and its direction of foreign trade.

Table 4.6. Tajikistan: Performance of Foreign Trade

	1993	1995	1997	1998	1999	2000	2001	2002
Merchandise Exports (Million US$)	456	839	746	597	689	784	652	737
Merchandise Imports (Million US$)	660	880	750	711	663	675	688	721
Unit value index for Exports	100	182	154	163	169	180	143	-
Unit value index for Imports	100	158	164	158	162	175	104	-
Terms of Trade (1993=100)	100	115	94	103	104	103	138	-
Trade Balance % GDP[a]	(29.4)	(7.8)	0.4	(8.6)	2.4	11.3	(3.4)	(1.5)
Exports % of GDP[a]	65.7	161.2	67.1	45.2	63.4	79.1	61.7	58.4 [b]
Imports % of GDP[a]	95.1	169.1	67.4	53.9	61.0	68.1	65.1	71.6 [b]

[a]GDP data for 1993 to 1998 are taken from EBRD (2000), 'Transition Report 2000'. The remainder come from ADB (2002a and 2004). [b] Also include services.

Source: ADB (2002a and 2004).

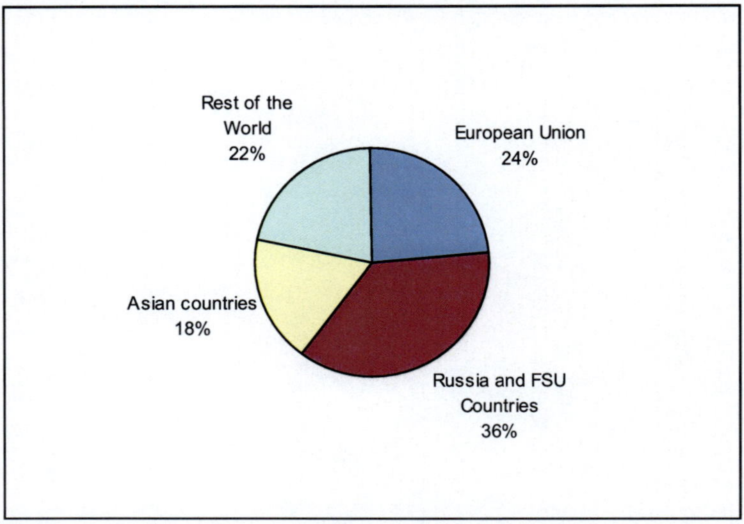

Figure 4.3. Tajikistan's Major Trading Partners in 2003

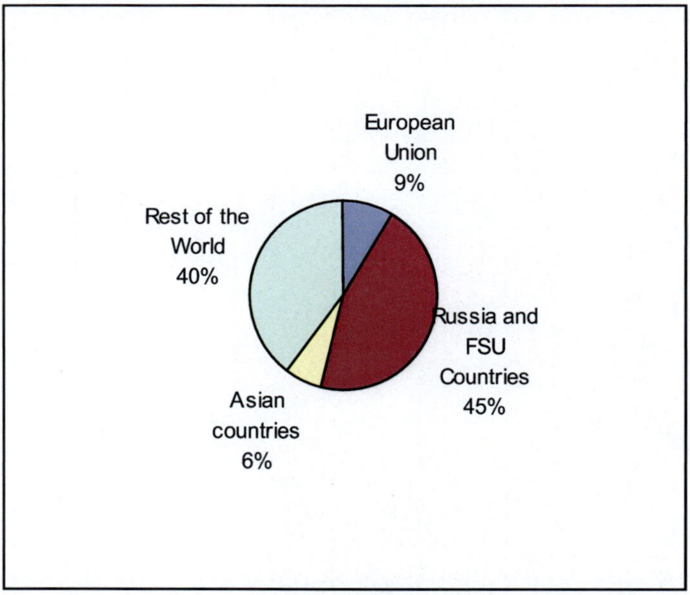

Figure 4.4. Tajikistan's Major Sources of Imports in 2003

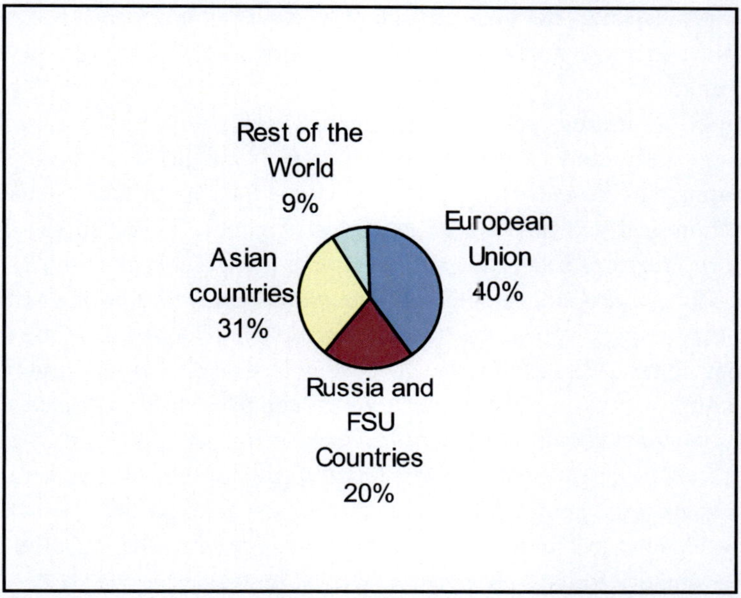

Figure 4.5. Major Destinations for Tajikistan's Exports in 2003

Tajikistan's exports are dominated by two major commodities, namely cotton and aluminium, which together account for over 70% share in export earnings. The third major export item is hydro-electricity. However, its share in the total exports has been falling. The excessive reliance on a few commodities makes the country's growth performance highly vulnerable to external shocks. Unpredictable weather conditions due to drought frequently influences cotton production, which contributes over one-fifth to the country's export earnings.

Over 90% of Tajikistan's imports are dominated by electricity, aluminium oxide, oil products and natural gas. It also relies on imports of grain and flour, but their shares in the country's total imports have been falling mainly due to an increase in wheat production. Wheat production increased mainly due to deregulation of agricultural input and output markets in late 1990s. Despite being an exporter of electricity, Tajikistan also import electricity as the generation of power is seasonal and the domestic grid network is not linked between the northern and southern regions of the country.

Despite abundant supplies of cotton and cheap labour, Tajikistan has only been able to process about 10% of its cotton into various types of textile products and carpets. There is a tremendous scope for garment and carpet production in the country, and this is an industry in which world trade is growing rapidly (Appendix

V). Improvements in business climate could significantly attract foreign investment in these sectors as Tajikistan enjoys GSP privileges in the US and European markets.

Tajikistan has not yet fully exploited its water resources, partly due to poor business climate and partly due to a monopoly of the state, in generating and distributing hydro-electricity. Deregulation of electricity generation and distribution grid will help attract foreign investment. Tajikistan has the potential to export its hydro-electricity not only to the Central Asian countries but also to China. The country's development in the long run depends on the performance of agricultural exports, given that the sector employs about 64% of the labour force and contributes 29% to GDP. However, due to the poor transport network within the country, processing and marketing of fruits have been restricted. As a result, despite abundant supplies of fruits, Tajikistan relies on imports of fruits and juices from Russia. Improvements in the internal transport network and some assistance in packaging will significantly reduce its reliance on imports of juice. In fact, with an improvement in internal and external transport networks it can be an exporter of juices and dry fruits.

Given the land-locked position and the weak physical infrastructure, both Kyrgyz Republic and Tajikistan's integration into the world trading system largely rely on cooperation from their neighbours in the areas of hydro-electricity, regional transport and cross-border procedures. The Central Asian nations in general should view regional cooperation as a means of achieving political and economic stability, as well as a forum to resolve issues relating to cross-border movements of goods and people. The current mechanisms for resolving issues relating to transport, power and water management remain problematic in the absence of a framework for regional cooperation. Although a number of regional agreements currently exist, as yet, very little progress is made due to the lack of political willingness. Appendix VI outlines engagement of CIS countries in international and regional arrangements. All CIS countries have a small domestic market and they lack resources to maintain transport networks as well as to utilize their natural resources effectively.

Table 4.7. FDI in Tajikistan and Direction of Foreign Trade

Item	1991	1992	1993	1994	1995	1996	1997	1998	1999	2000	2001	2002
FDI, net	-	8	9	12	20	25	30	24	21	19	9.5	36
External trade **(Mn US dollars: calendar year)**												
Exports, fob	-	185	456	559	839	770	746	597	689	784	652	737
Imports, cif	-	240	660	707	880	668	750	711	663	675	688	721
Trade balance	-	-55	-204	-148	-41	102	-4	-114	26	109	-36	16
Direction of trade **(Mn US dollars: calendar year)**												
Total exports	-	29.3	349.8	491.9	748.6	771.5	803.4	596.6	688.7	935.0	651.6	536.6
1. Netherlands	-	-	1.1	147.6	255.2	218.0	229.4	221.4	222.3	211.3	194.4	2.8
2. Uzbekistan	-	-	20.3	22.7	132.0	190.7	172.5	125.7	181.0	236.3	87.2	94.7
3. Russia	-	-	62.5	46.2	95.3	79.0	63.5	47.8	115.1	215.7	104.7	64.4
4. Switzerland	-	0.4	5.8	44.9	37.2	83.5	140.7	94.9	75.1	108.5	52.2	54.1
5. Kazakhstan	-	-	16.3	10.1	7.0	24.3	10.0	10.0	3.6	3.6		
6. Korea, Republic of	-	-	0.9	2.9	9.3	24.9	3.2	0.2	7.4	14.5		
7. Iran	-	-	-	1.4	0.7	1.7	3.5	13.6	13.5	13.5	29.9	24.8
8. Italy	-	6.8	2.5	0.4	2.4	6.6	7.8	9.8	5.1	11.6	5.8	18.9
9. Belgium	-	-	-	-	-	-	14.7	12.7	7.0	6.4	6.0	5.0
10.United Kingdom	-	-	119.9	30.3	20.7	15.2	6.5	5.1	5.5	7.1		

Table 4.7. (Continued)

Item	1991	1992	1993	1994	1995	1996	1997	1998	1999	2000	2001	2002
Total imports	-	72.9	532.1	547.0	809.9	668.1	750.3	711.0	663.1	800.9	687.5	704.5
1. Uzbekistan	-	-	65.4	83.2	251.4	198.9	261.6	227.3	264.4	301.6	150.7	163.6
2. Switzerland	-	0.1	4.3	100.4	51.7	99.8	185.1	157.9	25.1	31.7	2.1	2.1
3. Russia	-	-	83.8	60.7	136.0	74.4	115.1	102.2	92.4	61.5	129.4	88.0
4. Kazakhstan	-	-	65.5	32.8	26.5	52.4	42.0	51.9	78.8	105.7	89.1	96.7
5. United Kingdom	-	-	16.4	68.0	161.2	78.3	10.1	3.8	70.5	93.2	2.5	1.2
6. Ukraine	-	-	4.4	13.6	2.2	19.2	20.7	16.6	37.7	58.7	63.6	69.0
7. Turkmenistan	-	-	26.0	39.4	57.4	26.3	29.7	31.3	15.2	15.2	62.3	67.6
8. United States	-	9.7	8.7	31.9	25.3	16.0	3.2	32.8	1.7	15.7		
9. Iran	-	-	-	0.1	0.7	10.5	12.0	11.3	10.4	10.4	10.0	10.6
10. Azerbaijan	-	-	1.1	0.2	1.2	0.0	3.2	1.8	15.6	29.4	33.5	36.4

Source: FDI data comes from EBRD (2000) except for 2001 and 2002 which are taken from ADB (2003).Other data come from Asian Development Bank (2002c and 2003)

The cooperation should first begin by simplifying cross-border procedures for the movements of goods and people. The current procedures for regulating goods, vehicles and people between the countries have made international trade transactions very costly and time consuming. This has deterred investment, and discouraged export potential and employment growth in the region. Harmonization of tariff, cross-border procedures and documentary requirements will facilitate trade and investment.

Within the framework of the free trade area, each nation can have its own external tariffs, but they must be kept as low as possible to avoid trade diversion. In the context of free trade area if external tariffs are kept too high, it would be costly because of the diversion of trade from the most efficient supplier(s) to the least efficient supplier(s) located within the region. Also, in an environment where external tariffs are kept high it would attract tariff-jumping type foreign investment whose motive would be to capture the regional market rather than to utilize resources of comparative advantage. Also, currently, tight customs and border formalities are exercised in all neighbouring countries primarily to control smuggling, which hurts both trade and investment, and promotes rent-seeking behaviour.

CONCLUSION

Being small economies, both Kyrgyzstan and Tajikistan rely heavily on foreign trade as reflected by a high share of foreign trade in GDP. In both countries, exports and imports rose sharply since the early 1990s. However, this did not last long mainly due to the 1997 Russian Financial crisis, as Russia and other FSU countries were the major destinations for their exports. In Kyrgyz Republic, share of exports in GDP fell from about 39% in 1993 to 31% by 2001, reflecting a fall in purchasing power of the nation as a whole. As exports fell, imports also declined. Imports, which increased from US$448 million in 1993 to US$709 million in 1997, dropped to US$467 million by 2001. Kyrgyz Republic has a huge potential in hydro-electricity exports, but it has not fully exploited its water resources. Because of the climatic conditions, it also has potential in production and exports of vegetables.

After an initial decline in the immediate post-independence period, Tajikistan's exports rose from US$456 million in 1993 to US$839 million in 1995, then declined to US$652 million by 2001 mainly due to the Russian Financial crisis. A similar pattern was also observed in imports, which fell from US$880 million in 1995 to US$688 million in 2001. Despite fluctuations in exports, strong commodity prices contributed to an improvement in Tajikistan's terms of trade during 1993 to 2001. An improvement in terms of trade helped improve the current account deficit from about 18% of GDP in 1992 to 8% by 2001. Tajikistan's exports are dominated by two major commodities, namely, cotton and aluminium, which together account for over a 70% share in exports earnings. The country's third major export item is hydro-electricity, but its share in the total exports fell from 20% in 1996 to 12% by 2000 mainly due to inefficiency in the state-run electricity agency.

The Central Asia countries should view regional cooperation as a powerful tool for their growth and development. The possibility of regional cooperation among the Central Asian countries is very strong due to diversity in resources and similarity in culture among the countries. Apart from harmonization of cross-border procedures and tariffs, areas for cooperation should also include utilization of natural resources, and development of railways and road transport.

Chapter 5

DEVELOPMENT CHALLENGES OF KYRGYZ REPUBLIC AND TAJIKISTAN

INTRODUCTION

This chapter analyses development challenges of Kyrgyz Republic and Tajikistan following their independence from the FSU. While these challenges discussed in this chapter are specific to Kyrgyz Republic and Tajikistan, they are equally relevant to other Central Asian countries. The chapter is organised as follows. It begins with a discussion of development challenges of Kyrgyz Republic. Next, Tajikistan's development challenges are discussed. These challenges range from inefficient transport networks to cumbersome customs and cross-border formalities, and poor governance.

Kyrgyz Republic

Poor Physical Infrastructure

Kyrgyzstan mainly relies on road and rail networks for its international trade transactions. However, conditions of road networks are poor inside the country, and also throughout the region. Only about 40% of domestic road networks are paved in the country, making access from one region to another difficult in poor weather conditions. This has hindered the rural-urban integration and discouraged trade potential between the regions within the country. Like other Central Asia countries, access to international markets is a problem for Kyrgyzstan because of its land-locked position. For example, Russia is a major market for its exports of agricultural products but accessing to this market through Kazakhstan has been difficult. Poor access to international markets has significantly discouraged the export potential of agricultural products in which Kyrgyzstan has a comparative advantage. To overcome the international access problem, in recent years, it has used air cargos for exports of precious and semi-precious stones and gold, but it is expensive for bulky items. Efficient transport networks inside and outside the country are essential to facilitate trade and development.

Weak Institutions

Time consuming customs and cross-border formalities appears to be one of the major development challenges throughout Central Asian. In Kyrgyzstan traders are required to submit several documents obtained from different agencies for customs clearance which take a considerable amount of time and money. Significant delays occur at customs points as there are no automatic weighing and scanning machines, and goods are checked manually. The country's exports and imports have to go through at least two countries' territories (Kazakhstan and Uzbekistan) before reaching the final destination. The existing cross-border procedures for the movements of goods and people are costly and time consuming. For examples, at each country's entry and exit borders, consignments are checked. Consignments are even checked while goods are in transit. To avoid delays, shippers are forced to pay unofficial charges in several locations. Visa requirements, cross-border formalities and a transit permit contribute to delays and increase the costs of transportation. The official transit and entry fees vary from country to country, for example, it is US$0.70 per km in Uzbekistan. Even unloaded trucks have to pay the fees and very often returning trucks have no cargo, so all costs are borne by one shipper rather than shared between two or more (Molnar and Ojala, 2003). These restrictions and charges appear to have discouraged trade and investment. In the current situation, trade in vegetables in which Kyrgyzstan has a comparative advantage has not yet fully developed, because trade in such commodities demands better logistics, including trucks with refrigeration facilities and unrestricted access to the final destination.

Also, there are no trade promoting and supporting organizations in the country to promote domestic products in international markets, identify potential markets and establish links between exporters and importers. These services are essential for the development of the private sector. While there is a Chamber of Commerce, which is run by the state, it does not offer these services according to the needs of the private sector.

While basic documents used at border customs, such as export/import contracts and customs declaration forms, are common throughout Central Asia at each country's entry border they need to be filled in, signed and stamped in multi-copies for the use of each side of the border. In addition, official fees have to be paid at each border customs. Transit rules are often ignored as sealed consignments are checked in several places while goods are in transit despite the fact that all CIS countries have ratified a number of conventions regarding road and rail transportation (see Appendix VII). Clearly, the existing cross-border procedures are not consistent with the Revised Kyoto Convention nor do they satisfy the obligations of bilateral and multilateral agreements. Border formalities and customs fees vary between the countries despite the annual meeting of the Heads of State where they agree to harmonize procedures for deeper integration.

Governance and Transparency Issues

Governance and transparency is a real issue in all transitional economies and Kyrgyz Republic is no exception. There is a lack of coordination between departments and no 'one window system' exists where exporters and importers can obtain all required documents. Traders have to run from one department to another just to obtain documents to satisfy customs formalities. Also, exporters experience considerable delays in VAT refunds for which they are entitled. Getting VAT refunds take several months, which acts as a tax on exports in two ways. Firstly, due to inflation the value of refunds is much lower that what was paid. Secondly, exporters will keep on paying interest until they receive the full refund. For example, the annual inflation and interest rates are 14% and 10% respectively. An exporter is expecting a VAT refund of US$100. Due to red tape, he/she gets the refund in six months. Hence, the real value of the refund is US$88, after making allowance for interest paid and inflation. If one considers time spent in meeting VAT requirements, the actual refund is even lower than US$88. Delays in VAT refunds act as a tax on exporters. Poor governance and lack of transparency have made Kyrgyz Republic a least popular destination among the foreign investors in Central Asia (Appendix VIII). By 2002, gross foreign direct investment % of GDP was just over 1 % as against 12% for Kazakhastan and 3% for Tajikistan.

Weak institutions, poor governance and lack of transparency have contributed to a poor business environment in Kyrgyzstan. Table 5.1 presents snapshot of business environment in Kyrgyz Republic and compares it with the regional and OECD average. While entrepreneurs in Kyrgyzstan spend less days and less income in meeting official formalities compared with their counterparts in the region, the costs of enforcing contract in Kyrgyzstan is relatively higher. Also, time and cost required to resolve bankruptcies is higher in Kyrgyzstan than other countries. The recovery rate in Kyrgyzstan is 24.4 centscompared with the regional average of 30.5 cents and OECD averaged of 72.1 cents.

Table 5.1. Indicators of Business Environment in Kyrgyz Republic

	Kyrgyz Republic	Regional Average	OECD Average
Starting a Business (2004)			
Number of procedures	8	9	6
Time spend (days)	21	42	25
Cost (% of income per capita)	11.6	15.5	8.0
Hiring and Firing Workers (2004)			
Difficulty of Hiring Index	33	31.3	26.2
Rigidity of Hours Index	40	51.5	50.0
Difficulty of Firing Index	40	42.3	26.8
Rigidity of Employment Index	38	41.8	34.4
Firing Costs (weeks of wages)	21	38.3	40.4
Registering Property (2004)			
Number of Procedures	7	6	4
Time (days)	15	13	34
Cost (% of property per capita)	5.3	3.1	4.9
Getting Credit (2004)			
Cost to create collateral (% of income per capita)	12.4	7.7	5.2
Legal Right Index	8	5.4	6.3
Credit Information Index	0	2.0	5.0
Protecting Investors (2004)			
Disclosure Index	3	3.6	5.6
Enforcing Contracts (2004)			
Number of procedures	46	29	19
Time (days)	492	412	229
Cost (% of debt)	47.9	17.7	10.8
Closing a Business			
Time (years)	3.5	3.3	1.7
Cost (% of estate)	4	13.1	6.8
Recovery rate (cents per dollar)	24.4	30.5	72.1

Source: Downloaded from the World Bank website (Doingbusiness)

Rising Poverty and Inequality

A poor business environment resulted from inefficient institutions, infrastructure and poor governance has failed to encourage private sector participation in trade and investment, leading to lacklustre growth, high unemployment and rising poverty in the country. Table 5.2 presents poverty, inequality and the state of human development in Kyrgyzstan.

Table 5.2. Poverty, Inequality and Human Development in Kyrgyzstan

% of population below the national poverty line*		% of population below $2.15 per capita per day	Income Ratio of Highest 20% to Lowest 20%	Gini Co-efficient	Human Development Index			
1988	**1999**	**1999**	**2001**	**2001**	**1980**	**1990**	**2000**	**Rank in 2000**
37	55	49	4.2	0.32	na	na	0.712	102

*The national poverty line is defined as percentage of population earning a per capita income lower than the minimum consumption basket. For 1988, a per capita income of 75 rubles per month was used as the conventional poverty line

Source: IMF and World Bank (2002) for percentage of population below the national poverty line and percentage of people below $2.15 per capita per day. Other data come from ADB (2003)

A lack of sustainable growth, as a resulted of a poor business environment, has resulted in an increase of poverty and inequality in the country (Table 5.2). For instance, the percentage of people living below the poverty line has increased from 37% in 1988 to 55% by 1999. In terms of the human development index (HDI), Kyrgyzstan has one of the lowest rankings in the region after Tajikistan. As poverty, unemployment and inequality are on the rise cases of frequent crime and violence are common, in the country.

TAJIKISTAN

Poor Physical Infrastructure

While approximately 95% of commercial transactions use rail, the state rail service provider (Tajik Railways) suffers from several problems, including the shortages of wagons. The non-payments of dues to Kazak and Russian Railways have significantly limited the numbers of Russian wagons given to Tajik Railways. Due to the shortages of wagons at Tajik Railways, priority is given to exporters of aluminium and cotton, while exporters of other commodities have no choice, except for using road transport, which is costly and time consuming.

About 5% of international trade transactions take place by road, although conditions of road networks have been deteriorating throughout the region. Also, road conditions are poor inside the country and there are no regular transport services between the rural and urban areas. This has discouraged export potential of agricultural products. The rural population has very little commercial choice in disposing of their output or buying essential necessities. Even to go from one part of the country to another, Uzbekistan's territories have to be used. Access from the north to the south part of the country and vis-versa is impossible during the winter session.

Despite privatization of commercial transportation, its services have not improved in the absence of a well-developed private sector and the lack of finance. Intra-regional shipment of fruits, in which Tajikistan has a comparative advantage, requires better logistics, including trucks with refrigeration facilities and unrestricted access to the final destination. However, in the current environment trade in such a commodity has not developed.

Most of its exports and imports are high volume and using air transport is expensive. Thus, a negligible amount of trade transactions (0.5%) take place by air.

Telecommunications infrastructure is weak in Tajikistan. Per one thousand population are served by 36 lines and this has fallen from 45 lines in 1995 (ICT at a glance Tajikistan downloaded from the World Bank website). Access to the outside world is costly and difficult despite the operation of four private mobile phone companies and Internet providers. The cost of a three minutes call to US is US$8.16 in 2001 (ICT at a glance Tajikistan downloaded from the World Bank website). Internet access is extremely slow and costly. Poor Internet connections makes establishing links with potential buyers difficult and advertising Tajik products on the web expensive. In an environment where buying and selling decisions are frequently based on the Internet research and contact, not having easy access to the Internet means losing out on trade opportunities.

Weak Institutions

Customs procedures are time consuming and less transparent, creating uncertainty among traders. For example, any cargo can be declared suspicious and the clearance of such cargo takes a considerable amount of time and money. Depending on goods, exporters are required to produce at least five different documents, while importers are expected to produce seven documents. Customs clearance formalities can get worse if the consignment has to be opened and checked. Since there are no scanning and weighing machines at customs, inspections are done manually. Pilferage and damage often occur. Congestion at customs results in delay.

According to a study conducted by the Asian Development Bank in 2000, trade flows per customs staff are very low in Tajik customs, in comparison with other CIS countries. Annually each customs staff processes only about 65 customs declarations, indicating the poor productivity of customs. Lack of information about the customs policies and the rules have created uncertainty among importers and exporters, creating room for rent-seeking. Both exporters and importers are forced to pay unofficial fees to ensure that they meet the delivery target.

The country's land-locked position has made access to international markets costly and time consuming because of the visa requirements, transit permit systems and cross-border formalities. Visa and transit fees as well as cross-border formalities vary from country to country, despite the annual meeting of the Heads of State where they agree to harmonize the procedures for deeper integration. Each year Uzbekistan, Kazakhstan and Turkmenistan issue transit permits, which appear to be much lower than Tajikistan's requirements, leading to lower trade flows.

Tajik traders face additional problem in Uzbekistan because of the requirement to pay a 100% bond in US$ at the entry border which, in principle, is refunded at the exit border. But often there is a delay and the bonds are not refunded in US$. In case traders are unable to pay the bond, then an Uzbek customs official will accompany the consignment and there is a fee for this. In addition to official fees, unofficial charges have to be paid at each border customs. Shippers are forced to pay unofficial fees even in transit within the transit country. Clearly, the existing border procedures are not consistent with the Revised Kyoto Convention nor do they satisfy the obligations of bilateral and multilateral agreements.

Governance and Transparency Issues

There is no single agency or 'one window system' to facilitate trade, and exporters and importers are required to obtain several certificates from different departments. Each department charges fees for its services. Tajik customs do not even accept the quality certificate issued overseas; it must be obtained locally. Clearly, it creates an environment for rent-seeking.[1] Besides paying taxes, from time to time business houses are asked to make donations for celebrating official functions and this process in not transparent. While under the Duty Draw Back

---

[1] Red tape and complicated procedures do not generate revenue to government like tariffs, but benefits bureaucrats because they create an environment for corruption

Scheme, exporters are entitled for VAT refunds, it takes about one year to get the refunds. Also, enforcement of law and order is very weak and the protection of private property is a major concern among the business community.

Absence of Trade Promoting Organizations and Underdeveloped Banking System

There are no organizations that help identify potential markets, establish links between exporters and importers, and assist private sector with the packaging and labelling requirements. While there is a Chamber of Commerce in which the state has 51% share, it does not perform private sector development activities despite the fact that it has several full time staff, computer facility and Internet access. Clearly, absence of trade promoting and supporting organizations has hurt the production and exports of labour intensive goods in Tajikistan. At present several Tajik products do not meet the packaging and labelling requirement for a more demanding market. For example, Tajik apricot juice, is much cheaper than imported juice from Russia, but the local juice comes only in a two litre jar which is difficult to carry and store in the fridge. This has made the local product less attractive and hindered its export potential. Simply by improving the packaging and labelling of juice, its production and exports can significantly be increased. However, there is no institution to educate producers and assist them in packaging alternatives, labelling requirements and technology, and market information and contacts. There are several products whose exports can significantly be increased simply by improving packaging, design and maintaining contacts with potential buyers. Lack of trade supporting and promoting organizations has deterred the country's export potential.

The banking system is not yet fully developed in Tajikistan, although banks do provide some basic services. Most SMEs keep their money at home in US$ rather than in commercial banks because charges and taxes appear to be too high. A private sector businessman says 'it takes several days just to withdraw money from the bank and there are numerous charges'. This hurts international trade transactions and investment. Borrowing money from the banking system is extremely difficult as borrowers need to show 150% collateral security, which is not possible for most enterprises. Despite deregulation, interest rates remain very high (about 22% annually). Lack of finance has significantly deterred the growth prospects of textile and processed agricultural products which are labour intensive.

Rising Poverty and Inequality

Like other transitional economies, Tajikistan has also experienced lacklustre growth performance resulted from inefficient institutions, infrastructure and lack of law and order in the country. As a consequence, the government is not in a position to increase its investment in health, education and infrastructure which have been badly damaged by the civil war that lasted for about 7 years (until the mid 1990s). Also, lacklustre growth has contributed to rising unemployment, poverty, crime and violence. Poverty is very high and rising. As show in Table 5.3, the percentage of people living below the poverty line has increased from 59% in 1988 (before independence) to 83% in 1999 (post-independence). Not only poverty is high but also inequality is high, as measured by Gini Coefficient. In terms of HDI, Tajikistan was ranked in 112 place in 2000 (Table 5.3). The lower level of HDI is a reflection of the lower level of investment in health and education. Investment in health and education as percent of GDP has fallen from over 17% of GDP in the early 1990s to 3% by 1999.

Table 5.3. Poverty, Inequality and Human Development in Tajikistan

% of population below the national poverty line*		% of populatio n below $2.15 per capita per day	Income Ratio of Highest 20% to Lowest 20%	Gini Co-efficient	Human Development Index			
1988	**1999**	**1999**	**1998**	**1998**	**1980**	**1990**	**2000**	**Rank in 2000**
59	83	68	5.0	0.35	Na	0.74	0.667	112

*The national poverty line is defined as percentage of population earning a per capita income lower than the minimum consumption basket For 1988, a per capita income of 75 rubles per month was used as the conventional poverty line.

Source: IMF and World Bank (2002).

CONCLUSIONS

Development challenges faced by Kyrgyzstan and Tajikistan are very similar to the challenges faced by other transitional economies. These range from weak institutions, infrastructure, declining public investment and red-tape. The effective implementation of rule of law is also a major concern in transitional economies. These obstacles have contributed to a poor business environment leading to lacklustre growth, rising unemployment and poverty unless these challenges are addressed both Central Asian countries' transition to a market economy will be very costly.

Chapter 6

POLICY OPTIONS FOR KYRGYZ REPUBLIC AND TAJIKISTAN

INTRODUCTION

The purpose of this chapter is to outline policy options for Kyrgyz Republic and Tajikistan to tackle trade and development challenges with a view to facilitate trade and investment. This is crucial to accelerate growth, generate employment and alleviate poverty. It is in this context this chapter presents policy options which include regional cooperation, further reform and privatization of public enterprises, harmonization of cross-border formalities, and simplification of customs procedures. These measures should help facilitate trade and investment not only in Kyrgyz Republic and Tajikistan but also in other countries in the region.

TRADE AS AN ENGINE OF GROWTH

Trade is crucial for sustaining growth and alleviating poverty. Hence, attempts should be made to facilitate trade. Since these countries in Central Asia have an abundant supply of unskilled labour and they have a comparative advantage in goods and services that use unskilled labour intensively, removal of domestic/regional constraints, such as red tape, and improvements in supply-side rigidities, will increase the demand for unskilled labour. As demand for unskilled labour increases, it will help alleviate poverty by raising the real income of the poor and increasing the growth rate. A more rapid growth means more revenue, which will help the government to spend more on poverty alleviation programs and reduce reliance on external debts.

In this context, international integration is important for Kyrgyz Republic and Tajikistan for the following reasons. Firstly, removal of distortions allows resource allocation in line with their comparative advantage, which in turn enhances export potential. Export growth is an indirect way of increasing income and consumption and improving living standards. Secondly, foreign exchange earned through exports permits firms to import superior technologies and inputs, which improve efficiency. Thirdly, international integration, by enhancing export opportunities, allows firms to enjoy the benefits of large-scale production. Fourthly, increased exposure brought about by exporting and importing opportunities encourages firms to adopt best practices and maintain quality, leading to an improvement in efficiency. Fifthly, removal of distortion and greater international integration attract foreign investment, which helps create jobs and alleviates poverty. Foreign investment is essential for these countries because both countries are resource deficient, and they lack technology and marketing networks.

Being small economies, both Kyrgyzstan and Tajikistan rely heavily on foreign trade. In the former, foreign trade (exports and imports) as percentage of GDP is over 60%, while in the latter it is over 126% (in 2001), reflecting the importance of trade in growth and the standards of living. However, from year to year, there have been significant fluctuations in exports and imports in both countries, which appear to be mainly due to internal and regional rather than international factors. In both countries, after an initial decline, exports and imports rose sharply from mid 1990s. However, this did not last long mainly due to the 1997 Russian Financial crisis, as Russia and other FSU countries were the major destinations for their exports. While there is an enormous scope for trade expansion, as discussed earlier, the following measures are recommended.

Need For Further Reform and Privatization

Kyrgyz Republic has a huge potential in hydro-electricity production and exports, but it has not fully exploited its water resources. In fact, production and exports of electricity have been fluctuating and the country still imports electricity. This appears to be partly due to the poor pricing strategy and partly due to the poor management of the electricity authority. It appears that privatization of electricity production and distribution can significantly raise its production and exports. Because of the climatic conditions, Kyrgyzstan also has potential in production and exports of vegetables. However, exports of these commodities require just-in-time delivery. The provision of efficient transport facilities and minimum border and customs formalities can significantly increase its exports of vegetables to regional markets. Since these activities are labour intensive, they will help create employment opportunities. Kyrgyz Republic is endowed with pearls, precious and semi-precious stones and gold, these precious stones and metals are not processed into jewelleries, which could attract higher prices in international markets. Despite huge potential in hydro-electricity generation, Kyrgyzstan relies on imports of natural gas from Uzbekistan. Reform in the electricity authority and creation of suitable business environment might help increase the production of electricity and reduce reliance on imports of gas and other energy.

Tajikistan's exports are dominated by two major commodities, namely, cotton and aluminium, which together account for over a 70% share in export earnings. The country's third major export item is hydro-electricity, but its share in the total exports fell from 20% in 1996 to 12% by 2000. This appears to be mainly due to inefficiency in the state-run electricity agency. Despite being an exporter of electricity, Tajikistan also imports electricity. Deregulation of electricity generation and distribution will attract foreign investment and increase its production and exports of hydro-electricity.

Tajikistan has only been able to process about 10% of its cotton into various types of textile products and carpets despite abundant supplies of cotton and cheap labour. There is a tremendous scope for garments and carpet production in the country. Despite abundant supplies of fruits, processing and marketing of fruits have been deterred due to the poor transport network within the country. Improvements in the internal transport network and privatization of rail services can facilitate exports of juices and dry fruits.

The effective implementation of privatization and competition policy can help improve competitiveness of business community in Kyrgyz Republic and Tajikistan. While the electricity sector has been open as a joint venture company in Tajikistan, the state control remains significant. Hence, the price of electricity is not yet fully deregulated. Likewise, the State still maintains control over roads and railways. Privatization of electricity, roads and railways has to proceed as quickly as possible to improve economy-wide efficiency. The culture of subsidizing energy, gas and electricity hurts the private sector in two ways. Firstly, governments will have to collect additional resources, which are most likely to come from export-import taxes. Secondly, subsidized energy means an incentive to use capital-intensive technology in a labour abundant country. In Tajikistan, agriculture sector reform has shown positive signs in terms of output, exports and productivity growth. The long-term strategy should be to keep the sector competitive and sustain growth, which requires privatization of irrigation services.

Regional Cooperation

All Central Asian nations, including Kyrgyz Republic and Tajikistan should view regional cooperation as a means of achieving political and economic stability, as well as a forum to resolve issues relating to cross-border movements of goods and people. Regional cooperation can also resolve transport, electricity, gas and water issues that create tension between the neighbours from time to time. All CIS countries have a small domestic market and lack resources to maintain transport networks as well as to utilize their resources effectively, namely, electricity, mining, agriculture and manufacturing. In this context, regional cooperation can be a powerful mechanism and it should be viewed as an opportunity rather than a threat.

Regional cooperation can also be a powerful tool in gaining experience in export production and marketing. Having a closed economy for a long time, these countries lack experience in these areas, which are essential ingredients for a market economy. Regional cooperation will provide them with these experiences in familiar regional markets before going into a complex global market. However, such strategies should be consistent with the aim of global integration in the long-term. Hence, regional cooperation should be seen as a means of achieving these experiences as well as developing infrastructure.

The cooperation should first begin by simplifying cross-border procedures for the movements of goods and people. The current procedures for regulating goods, vehicles and people between the countries have made international trade transactions very costly and time consuming. This has deterred investment and discouraged export potential and employment growth in the region. Harmonization of tariff, cross-border procedures and documentary requirements will help facilitate trade and investment.

Within the framework of the free trade area, each nation can have its own external tariffs, but they must be kept as low as possible to avoid trade diversion. It is also advisable to keep external tariffs close to each other's rates, which can significantly reduce smuggling of imported goods from the low to the high tariff countries. Currently, tight customs and border formalities are exercised in all neighbouring countries primarily to control smuggling, which hurts both trade and investment, and promotes rent-seeking behaviour.

A similar external tariff structure may look a bit ambitious in the current regional environment because Kyrgyz Republic and Tajikistan have very low tariffs (average 5%), while Kazakhstan has moderate tariffs, and Uzbekistan and Russia have relatively high tariffs. Being a member of WTO, Kyrgyzstan cannot go back to a high tariff regime and Uzbekistan and Russia may not like to reduce their tariffs closer to Kyrgyzstan's level. Since both Uzbekistan and Russia are in the WTO accession process, international and regional institutions should actively engage in policy dialogues with these countries to bring barriers down at least closer to Kazakhstan. Linking development assistance with liberalization commitments can also help to achieve this goal.

Regional cooperation among the Central Asian countries is feasible due to diversity in resources and similarity in culture among the countries. Apart from harmonization of cross-border procedures for the movement of goods and people, areas for cooperation should also include utilization of natural resources, and development of railways and road transport.

GOOD GOVERNANCE

To facilitate global integration, good governance and transparency are crucial as discussed in Chapter 1. While tariffs have been significantly reduced in both Kyrgyz Republic and Tajikistan and they do not apply non-tariff barriers, there are several procedural barriers that hinder trade (Chapter 4). Simplification of documentary requirements and a provision of 'one-window system' for export/import formalities can help facilitate trade in both Kyrgyzstan and Tajikistan. Also, an introduction of the pre-shipment inspection system will help expedite exports by reducing the need for checking cargo in several locations inside the country. There is an urgent need for the enforcement of law and order and protection of private property.

In both Kyrgyz Republic and Tajikistan, the growth prospects of private sector development have been hindered due to the absence of trade promoting organizations that help identify potential markets, provide market information, and establish links with potential buyers. While there is a Chamber of Commerce in both countries, they do not provide these services. Creation of a Trade Promotion Centre in the private sector and privatization of the Chamber of Commerce to make its services customer-oriented can help develop the private sector.

Harmonization of tariffs, cross-border procedures and customs documentation is another area for reform. Since each Central Asian country has different tariffs and customs duties, prices of imported goods vary between the countries, creating an environment for smuggling of imported goods from the low to the high tariff countries. To control this, tight border formalities are currently exercised. Even inside the country, several checks are performed, and documents are checked and re-checked at customs. Harmonization of tariffs will reduce the need for such stringent formalities.

Also, there is a need to harmonize cross-border procedures for the movements of people and goods, including documentary requirements, which will help facilitate trade and help attract foreign investment. The Revised Kyoto Convention adopted by the World Customs Organization (WCO) Council in 1999 is an important step in this direction. It places greater emphasis on transparency, simplicity and predictability of customs procedures.

Reform in Foreign Investment Policy

Apart from the poor business climate, weakness in policy regime appears to have discouraged employment intensive foreign investment and have made poverty alleviation a difficult task. For example, incentives for foreign investment are based on the amount of capital invested rather than numbers of jobs created. This appears to have discouraged employment intensive foreign investment, particularly in the processing of agricultural products (in both Kyrgyzstan and Tajikistan) as well as carpets and garments in Tajikistan. Since these countries have an abundant labour supply, offering incentives based on the number of jobs created can attract employment intensive foreign investment. This will help reduce unemployment and alleviate poverty. Hence there is an urgent need to amend the Foreign Investment Law to encourage labour intensive investment.

Conclusion

Development challenges faced by the Central Asian countries in general and Kyrgyz Republic and Tajikistan in particular are identical. This is because all Central Asian countries were under the FSU until 1991, and lack efficient institutions and infrastructure to manage international integration. Also they all are land-locked. In this context, Central Asian nations should view regional cooperation as a means of achieving political and economic stability, as well as a forum to resolve issues relating to cross-border movements of goods and people.

Regional cooperation can also resolve transport, electricity, gas and water issues that create tension between the neighbours from time to time. All CIS countries have a small domestic market and lack resources to maintain transport networks as well as to utilize their resources effectively, namely, electricity, mining, agriculture and manufacturing. In this context, regional cooperation can be a powerful mechanism and it should be viewed as an opportunity rather than a threat.

The cooperation should first begin by simplifying cross-border procedures for the movements of goods and people. The current procedures for regulating goods, vehicles and people between the countries have made international trade transactions very costly and time consuming. This has deterred investment and discouraged export potential and employment growth in the region. Harmonization of tariff, cross-border procedures and documentary requirements will help facilitate trade and investment.

Within the framework of the free trade area, each nation can have its own external tariffs, but they must be kept as low as possible to avoid trade diversion. It is also advisable to keep external tariffs close to each other's rates, which can significantly reduce smuggling of imported goods from the low to the high tariff countries. Currently, tight customs and border formalities are exercised in all neighbouring countries primarily to control smuggling, which hurts both trade and investment, and promotes rent-seeking behaviour.

There is also an urgent need for privatization of public enterprises, effective enforcement of law and order, and development of internal transport network. The simplification of official formalities and customs procedures is also crucial to facilitate growth and development.

Appendix I
Socio-Economic Indicators of Kyrgyzstan

People	1999 2002 2003
Population, total	4.9 million 5.0 million 5.1 million
Population growth (annual %)	1.4 1.0 1.0
National poverty rate (% of population)	64.1
Life expectancy (years)	67.0 65.2
Fertility rate (births per woman)	2.6 2.4
Infant mortality rate (per 1,000 live births)	52.0
Under 5 mortality rate (per 1,000 children)	61.0

Births attended by skilled health staff (% of total)	--
Child malnutrition, weight for age (% of under 5)	--
Child immunization, measles (% of under 12 mos)	99.0 98.0
Prevalence of HIV (female, % ages 15-24)	--
Primary completion rate, total (% age group)	--
Primary completion rate, female (% age group)	--
Net primary enrollment (% relevant age group)	81.9
Environment	
Surface area (sq. km)	199.9 thousand 199.9 thousand
Forests (1,000 sq. km)	--
Deforestation (avearge annual % 1990-2000)	--
Freshwater resources per capita (cubic meters)	9,292.6
CO2 emissions (metric tons per capita)	1.0
Access to improved water source (% of total pop.)	--
Access to improved sanitation (% of urban pop.)	--
Energy use per capita (kg of oil equivalent)	504.6
Electricity use per capita (kWh)	1,511.4

Economy

GNI, Atlas method (current US$)	1.4 billion
	1.4 billion
	1.6 billion
GNI per capita, Atlas method (current US$)	300.0
	290.0
	330.0
GDP (current $)	1.2 billion
	1.6 billion
	1.7 billion
GDP growth (annual %)	3.7
	-0.5
	5.3
GDP implicit price deflator (annual % growth)	37.6
	2.3
	4.0
Value added in agriculture (% of GDP)	37.7
	37.8
	39.2
Value added in industry (% of GDP)	26.7
	23.4
	23.2
Value added in services (% of GDP)	35.6
	38.9
	37.6
Exports of goods and services (% of GDP)	42.2
	39.6
	42.1

Imports of goods and services (% of GDP)	57.0 43.4 46.4
Gross capital formation (% of GDP)	18.0 17.6 17.5
Current revenue, excluding grants (% of GDP)	15.8
Overall budget balance, including grants (% of GDP)	-2.4

Technology and infrastructure

Fixed lines and mobile telephones (per 1,000 people)	76.9 87.9
Telephone average cost of local call (US$ per three minutes)	0.1
Personal computers (per 1,000 people)	12.7
Internet users	10,000.0 152.0 thousand
Paved roads (% of total)	91.1
Aircraft departures	8,300.0 4,000.0

Trade and finance

Trade in goods as a share of GDP (%)	84.4 67.1
Trade in goods as a share of goods GDP (%)	125.9 99.3

High-technology exports (% of manufactured exports)	5.5 5.7
Foreign direct investment, net inflows in reporting country (current US$)	44.4 million 4.8 million
Present value of debt (current US$)	1.3 billion
Total debt service (% of exports of goods and services)	20.4 25.3
Short-term debt outstanding (current US$)	60.7 million 18.5 million
Aid per capita (current US$)	58.2 37.2

Source: World Development Indicators database, August 2004

APPENDIX II
SOCIO-ECONOMIC INDICATORS OF TAJIKISTAN

People	1999 2002 2003
Population, total	6.2 million 6.3 million 6.3 million
Population growth (annual %)	0.5 0.6 0.6
Life expectancy (years)	66.6
Fertility rate (births per woman)	2.9
Infant mortality rate (per 1,000 live births)	90.0
Under 5 mortality rate (per 1,000 children)	116.0
Births attended by skilled health staff (% of total)	--

Child immunization, measles (% of under 12 mos)	79.0 84.0
Prevalence of HIV (female, % ages 15-24)	--
Literacy total (% of ages 15 and above)	99.1
Literacy female (% of ages 15 and above)	--
Primary completion rate, total (% age group)	--
Primary completion rate, female (% age group)	--
Net primary enrollment (% relevant age group)	96.3
Net secondary enrollment (% relevant age group)	--
Environment	
Surface area (sq. km)	143.1 thousand 143.1 thousand
Forests (1,000 sq. km)	--
Deforestation (avearge annual % 1990-2000)	--
Freshwater resources per capita (cubic meters)	12.705.5
CO2 emissions (metric tons per capita)	0.8
Access to improved water source (% of total pop.)	--
Access to improved sanitation (% of urban pop.)	--
Energy use per capita (kg of oil equivalent)	542.9
Electricity use per capita (kWh)	2.161.9

Economy

GNI, Atlas method (current US$)	1.1 billion 1.1 billion 1.2 billion
GNI per capita, Atlas method (current US$)	170.0 170.0 190.0
GDP (current $)	1.1 billion 1.2 billion 1.3 billion
GDP growth (annual %)	3.7 9.5 10.2
GDP implicit price deflator (annual % growth)	26.5 21.6 9.9
Value added in agriculture (% of GDP)	27.4 29.4 23.4
Value added in industry (% of GDP)	23.4 24.7 20.2
Value added in services (% of GDP)	49.2 45.9 56.4
Exports of goods and services (% of GDP)	64.2 64.4 60.0

Imports of goods and services (% of GDP)	65.7 77.8 79.3
Gross capital formation (% of GDP)	17.3 18.0 19.0
Current revenue, excluding grants (% of GDP)	10.2
Overall budget balance, including grants (% of GDP)	-0.8
Technology and infrastructure	
Fixed lines and mobile telephones (per 1,000 people)	34.9 39.3
Telephone average cost of local call (US$ per three minutes)	0.0 0.0
Internet users	2.000.0 3.500.0
Paved roads (% of total)	--
Aircraft departures	3.800.0 5.900.0
Trade and finance	
Trade in goods as a share of GDP (%)	124.5 119.9
Trade in goods as a share of goods GDP (%)	208.3 152.7

High-technology exports (% of manufactured exports)	--
Foreign direct investment, net inflows in reporting country (current US$)	21.0 million 8.7 million
Present value of debt (current US$)	898.0 million
Total debt service (% of exports of goods and services)	11.3 9.3
Short-term debt outstanding (current US$)	101.9 million 59.9 million
Aid per capita (current US$)	19.9 26.9

Source: World Development Indicators database, August 2004

APPENDIX III
THE GENERAL AGREEMENT ON TARIFF AND TRADE (GATT 1947)

ARTICLE V. FREEDOM OF TRANSIT

1. Goods (including baggage), and also vessels and other means of transport, shall be deemed to be in transit across the territory of a contracting party when the passage across such territory, with or without transhipment, warehousing, breaking bulk, or change in the mode of transport, is only a portion of a complete journey beginning and terminating beyond the frontier of the contracting party across whose territory the traffic passes. Traffic of this nature is termed article 'traffic in transit'.
2. There shall be freedom of transit through the territory of each contracting party, via the routes most convenient for international transit, for traffic in transit to or from the territory of other contracting parties. No distinction shall be made which is based on the flag of vessels, the place of origin, departure, entry, exit or destination, or any circumstances relating to the ownership of goods, of vessels or other means of transport.
3. Any contracting party may require that traffic in transit through its territory be entered at the proper custom house, but, except in cases of failure to comply with applicable customs laws and regulations, such traffic coming from or going to the territory of other contracting parties shall not be subject to any unnecessary delays or restrictions and shall be exempt from customs duties and from all transit duties or other charges imposed in respect of transit, except charges for transportation or those commensurate with administrative expenses entailed by transit or with the cost of services rendered.

4. All charges and regulations imposed by the contracting parties or traffic in transit to or from the territory of other contracting parties shall be reasonable, having regard to the conditions of the traffic.
5. With respect to all charges, regulations and formalities in connection with transit, each contracting party shall accord to traffic in transit to or from the territory of any other contracting party treatment no less favourable than the treatment accorded to traffic in transmit to or from any third country.
6. Each contracting party shall accord to products which have been in transit through the territory of any other contracting party treatment no less favourable that that which would have been accorded to their destination without going through the territory of such other contracting party.
7. The provisions of this Article shall not apply to the operation of aircraft in transit, but shall apply to air transit goods (including baggage).

Source: World Trade Organization, (1994), *Results of the Uruguay Round*, Geneva, pp 492-493 and p.545

APPENDIX IV

BUSINESS CLIMATE IN THE CAUCASUS, CENTRAL ASIA, RUSSIA, UKRAINE, BELARUS AND MOLDOVA OBSTACLES TO DOING BUSINESS; CAUCASUS, CENTRAL ASIAN, AND THE SLAVIC REPUBLICS' RATINGS AMONG 22 WORLD REGIONS

The Region's ranking out of 22 world regions in Brunetti et al 2001	The Caucasus Region	The Central Asian Region	Russia, Ukraine, Belarus and Moldova
Total obstacles	**8**	**19**	**21**
Labour, price and environmental regulations and regulations for starting a business	2	3	5
Inflation and financing related obstacles	5	16	14
Trade and exchange rate related obstacles	11	20	21
Public revenue and expenditure policies related	11	20	18
Uncertainty related obstacles (Policy instability, costs)	16	21	22
Crime related obstacles	11	14	18

(1 = Lowest; 22 = Highest Obstacle Rating)

Source: Molnar and Ojala, (2003), (Original source: A. Brunetti, G. Kisunko, A. Weder (2001), 'How business see government responses from private sector surveys', *IFC Discussion Paper No. 33.*)

Appendix V
Export Value Growth and Share in Total Exports[A] of the 20 Most Market-Dynamic Products, 1980-1998 (Per Cent)

SITC code	Product group	Average annual export value growth	Share in total world exports		Share in total exports from developing countries	
		1980-1998	**1980**	**1998**	**1980**	**1998**
776	Transistors and semiconductors	16.3	1.0	4.0	1.9	7.7
752	Computers	15.0	0.9	3.4	0.2	5.9
759	Parts of computers and office machines	14.6	0.7	2.3	0.3	3.6
871	Optical instruments	14.1	0.1	0.3	0.0	0.3
553	Perfumery and cosmetics	13.3	0.2	0.5	0.1	0.2
261	Silk	13.2	0.0	0.0	0.0	0.0
846	Knitted undergarments	13.1	0.3	0.6	0.8	1.4
893	Plastic articles	13.1	0.6	1.2	0.6	1.1
771	Electric power machinery	12.9	0.3	0.6	0.2	0.8
898	Musical instruments and records	12.6	0.3	0.7	0.2	0.5
612	Leather manufactures	12.4	0.1	0.1	0.1	0.2

111	Non-alcoholic beverages	12.2	0.1	0.1	0.1	
872	Medical instruments	12.1	0.2	0.4	0.1	0.1
773	Electricity distribution					0.2
	equipment	12.0	0.4	0.7	0.3	
764	Telecommunications	11.9	1.5	3.0	1.7	1.0
	equipment and parts	11.9	0.2	0.3	0.8	2.9
844	Textile undergarments	11.9	0.2	0.4	0.1	0.8
048	Cereal preparations	11.7	0.2	0.3	0.1	0.2
655	Knitted fabrics	11.6	1.1	2.0	0.4	0.6
541	Pharmaceutical products	11.5	1.1	1.7	0.7	0.6
778	Electrical machinery	12.9	9.5	22.6	14.1	1.5
						28.7
	20 most dynamic products					
	***Memo Item*:**					
	World exports[b]	8.4				
	Developing country					
	exports[b]	11.3	15.4	24.3		

Note: SITC code numbers refer to Standard International Trade Classification, Revision 2.

[a.] Excluding fuels.

[b.] Total of all product groups.

Source: Trade and Development Report, (2002), Part II UN: NY & Geneva.

APPENDIX VI
ENGAGEMENT OF CIS-5 COUNTRIES IN INTERNATIONAL AND REGIONAL ARRANGEMENTS

	WTO Status and date of membership[a]	IMF trade rating[b]	ECO[c]	EURASEC[d]	SCO[e]	CAEU[f]	SPECA[g]	CAF[h]
Kazakhstan	Observer	--	Yes	Yes	Yes	Yes	Yes	Yes
Kyrgyz Republic	Dec. 1998	1.	Yes	Yes	Yes	Yes	Yes	Yes
Tajikistan	Observer	1.	Yes	Yes	Yes	Yes	Yes	Yes
Turkmenistan	--	--	Yes				Yes	
Uzbekistan	Observer	9.	Yes		Yes	Yes	Yes	Yes

Note:

[a] WTO membership data: www.wto.org, read Nov. 11, 2002.

[b] IMF rating of 1 is the most liberal category. Rating of 10 is the least liberal category. *Source* IMF, www.imf.org.

[c] Economic Cooperation Organization. Pakistan, Iran and Turkey are also members.

[d] Eurasia Economic Community also include Russia and Belarus.

[e] Shanghai Cooperation Organization. China and Russia are also members.

[f] Central Asian Economic Union.

[g] UN Special Program for the Economies of Central Asia. Kazakhstan is leading the Project Working Group on Transport of SPECA.

[h] Central Asia Forum.

Source: With some modifications taken from Molnar and Ojala (2003)

APPENDIX VII
THE MAIN INTERNATIONAL ROAD AND RAIL TRANSPORT AGREEMENTS AND CONVENTIONS RATIFIED BY CIS-5, AS OF FEBRUARY 15, 2002

Category (No. of conventions)	Convention or agreement with the year of establishment	Kazakhstan	Kyrgyz Rep.	Tajikistan	Turkmenistan	Uzbekistan
Infrastructure networks (6)	European road network (AGR), 1975	X				
	European rail networks (AGC), 1985					
	European rail networks (AGC), 1985					
Road traffic (11)	Road traffic, 1949 and 1968	X	X	X	X	X
	Road signs and signals, 1968, with 1971 supplements		X	X	X	X
	Protocol road markings, 1973					
Road transport (9)	Work of crews international road transport (AETR) 1970	X			X	X
	Contract road goods transport (CMR), 1956, with protocol to CMR, 1978	X	X	X	X	X
Border crossing facilitation (14)	TIR Convention, 1975	X	X	X	X	X
	Temporary imported commercial vehicles, 1956		X			
	Customs container convention, 1972					X
	Harmonization of frontier control of goods, 1982		X			X

Dangerous goods and special cargoes (5)	Dangerous goods by roads (ADR), 1957	X				
	Perishable foodstuffs (ATP), 1970	X				X

Source: Molnar and Ojala, (2003), (Original *source*: UNECE (2002), 'The facilitation in a global trade environment, Note by the Secretariat', UNCEE; TRADE/2002/21/21 March 2002)

APPENDIX VIII
INTEGRATION WITH THE GLOBAL ECONOMY: CENTRAL ASIAN COUNTRIES IN THE GLOBAL CONTEXT

	Trade in goods				Ratio of commercial service exports to merchandise exports		Growth in real trade less growth in real GDP	Gross private capital flows		Gross foreign direct investment	
	% of GDP		% of Goods GDP		%		Percentage points	% of GDP		% of GDP	
	1990	**2002**	**1990**	**2002**	**1990**	**2002**	**1990-2002**	**1990**	**2002**	**1990**	**2002**
Kazakhstan	-	65.8	-	128.9	-	14.8	-3.0	-	34.2	-	12.3
Kyrgyz Republic	-	67.1	-	99.3	-	24.3	-2.1	-	11.6	-	1.4
Tajikistan	-	119.9	-	152.7	-	8.2	-	-	10.6	-	3.0
Turkmenistan	-	70.4	-	-	-	-	3.8	-	-	-	-
Uzbekistan	-	80.0	-	130.5	-	-	-1.2	-	-	-	-
World	32.5 w	40.3 w	80.2 w	116.0 w	21.5	23.1 w		10.1 w	20.8 w	2.7 w	6.0 w
Low income	26.9	37.3	-	-	14.6	19.4		3.0	4.4	0.5	1.7
Middle income	35.2	54.9	74.6	116.8	16.5	15.6		6.8	12.4	1.0	3.7
Low and middle income	33.4	51.8	74.5	115.0	16.2	16.1		6.0	11.1	0.9	3.3
High income	32.3	37.6	80.9	*117.2*	23.2	25.5		10.9	22.9	3.0	6.6

Note: w refers to weighted averages
Source: World Bank, (2004).

BIBLIOGRAPHY

ADB. (2002a), *Key Indicators of Developing Asian and Pacific Countries*, ADB: Manila.

ADB. (2002b), Asian Development Outlook, ADB: Manila.

ADB. (2002c), *Key Indicators 2001: Growth and Change in Asia and the Pacific Countries,* (New York: OUP, 2001).

ADB. (2003), '*Key Indicators 2003: Growth and Change in Asia and the Pacific Countries',* (New York: OUP, 2003).

ADB. (2004), *Asian Development Outlook*, ADB: Manila.

Ahluwalia, I. J. (1991), *Productivity and Growth in Indian Manufacturing,* Delhi: Oxford University Press.

Akrasanee, N. and Wiboonchutikula, P. (1994), 'Trade and Industrialization Policy and Productivity Growth in Thailand' in G. K. Helleiner (ed.), *Trade and Industrialization in Turbulent Times,* New York: Routledge, pp 421-452.

Balassa, B. (1967), *Trade Liberalization Among Industrial Countries: Objectives and Alternatives*, New York: McGraw Hill.

Balassa, B. (1978), 'Export Incentives and Export performance in Developing Countries: A Comparative Analysis', *Weltwirtschaftliches*, 114 (1), pp 24-59.

Balassa, B. (1982), *Development Strategies in Semi-industrial Economies*, Baltimore: Johns Hopkins University Press.

Balassa, B. (1988), 'Export and Growth: The Lessons of East *Asian Development: An Overview',* Economic Development and Cultural Change, 36 (3), pp S273-S290.

Balla, S. (2002), *Imaging There's No Country Poverty, Inequality and Growth in the Era of Globalization*, Washington: Institute for International Economics.

Batchelor, R.A., Major, R.L. and Morgan, A.D. (1980), *Industrialization and the Basis for Trade, Cambridge*: Cambridge University Press.

Banerji, R. and Riedel, J. (1980), Industrial Employment Expansion Under Alternative Trade Strategies: Case of India and Taiwan, *Journal of Development Economics*, 7, pp 567-377.

Bergsman, J. (1974), 'Commercial Policy, Allocative Efficiency and X-efficiency', *Quarterly Journal of Economics,* 88 (3), pp 409-433.

Bhagwati, J. (1978), *Foreign Trade Regimes and Economic Development: Anatomy and Consequences of Foreign Exchange Control Regimes*, Cambridge: Ballinger Publishing Company.

Bhagwati, J.N. (1982), 'Directly Unproductive Profit Seeking (DUP) Activities', *Journal of Political Economy*, 90 (5), pp 988-1002.

Bhagwati, J. N. (1988), '*Export-Promoting Trade Strategy: Issues and Evid*ence', World Bank Research Observer, 3 (1), pp 27-58.

Bhagwati, J. N. and Desai P. (1970), *Planning for Industrialization*, London: Oxford University Press.

Bhagwati and Srinivashan, (1988), 'Revenue seeking: A Generalisation of Theory of Tariff', *Journal of Political Economy*, 88, pp 1069-1087.

Bonelli, R. (1992), 'Growth and Productivity in Brazilian Industries Impact of Trade Orientation', *Journal of Development Economics*, 39, pp 85-109.

Brunetti, A., Kisunko, G., and Weder, A. (2001), 'How business see government responses from private sector surveys', *IFC Discussion Paper* No. 33.

Bourguignon, F. and Morrison, C. (1989), *External Trade and Income Distribution,* Paris: Development Centre of the Organization for Economic Cooperation and Development.

Brown, F. and Dominguez, F. (1994), 'The Dynamics of Productivity Performance in Mexican Manufacturing, 1984-90', *The Developing Economies*, XXXII (3), pp 279-298.

Chen, T. (1987), 'Comparing Technical Efficiency Between Import-substitution-oriented and Export-oriented Foreign Firms in a Developing Economy', *Journal of Development Economics*, 26, pp 277-289.

Chen, T. and Tang D. (1990), 'Export Performance and *Productivity Growth: The Case of Taiwan', Economic* Development and Cultural Change, 38 (3), pp 575-85.

Chenery, H., Robinson, S. and Syrquin, M. (1986), *Industrialization and Growth: A Comparative Study*, New York: Oxford University Press.

Chenery, H.B. (1980), 'Interactions Between Industrialization and Exports', *American Economic Review*, pp 281-287.

Corden W. M. (1987), 'Protection and Liberalization: A Review of Analytical Issues', *IMF Occasional Paper*, Working Paper No. 54.

Dollar, D. and Sokoloff, K. (1990), 'Patterns of Productivity Growth in South Korea Manufacturing Industries, 1963-1979', *Journal of Development Economics*, 33, pp 309-327.

Dornbusch, R. (1992), 'The Case for Trade Liberalization in Developing Countries', *Journal of Economic Perspectives*, 6, pp 69-85.

Drabek, Z. and Laird (1997), The New Liberalism: Trade policy in transition and their integration in the multilateral trading system' (processed), WTO, Geneva.

EBRD, (2002), *'Transition Report 2002'*.

EBRD, (2000), *'Transition Report 2000'*.

EBRD, (1999), *'Transition Report'* (various issues). EBRD: London.

Esfasani, H. S. (1991), 'Export, Imports and Economic Growth in Semi-industrialized Countries', *Journal of Development Economics*, 35, pp 93-116.

Fujita, N. (1994), 'Liberalization Policies and Productivity in India', *The Developing Economies,* XXXII (4), pp 509-524.

Gleason, G. (2003), *Market and Politics in Central Asia* , Routledge: London.

Golder, B. N. (1985), *Productivity Growth in Indian Industry*, New Delhi: Allied Publishers Private Limited.

Greenaway, D. and Nam, C. H. (1988), *'Industrialization and Macroeconomic Performance in Developing Countries under Alternative Trade Strategies'*, Kyklos, 41, pp 419-435.

Handoussa, H. M., Nishimizu, M. and Page, J. M. (1986), 'Productivity Change in Egyptian Public Sector Industry After The Opening 1973-79', *Journal of Development Economics,* 20, pp 53-73.

Harrison, A. E. (1994), 'Productivity, Imperfect Competition and Trade Reform Theory and Evidence', *Journal of International Economics*, 36, pp 534-573.

Havrylyshyn, O. (1990), *'Trade Policy and Productivity Gains in Developing Countries: A Survey of the Literature'*, World Bank Research Observer, 5 (1), pp 1-24.

Hsia, M. W. (1987), 'Test of Causality and Exogeneity Between Exports and Economic Growth: The Case of the Asian NICs', *Journal of Economic Development,* 12 (2), pp 143-159.

IMF and World Bank, (2002), *Poverty Reduction, Growth and Debt Sustainability in Low Income CIS Countries*, Memoe.

IMF. *(2000),* 'Kyrgyz Republic: Selected Issues and Statistical Appendix', IMF: Washington D. C.

IMF. (1992a), *World Economic and Financial Survey*, IMF, Washington.

IMF. (2003), *'Kyrgyz Republic: Selected Issues and Statistical Appendix'*, IMF: Washington D. C.

Kajiwara, H. (1994), 'The Effect of Trade and Foreign Investment Liberalization Policy on Productivity in the Philippines', *The Developing Economies,* XXXII (4), pp 492-508.

Kaldor, N. (1967), *Strategic Factors in Economic Development*, New York: W. F. Humphrey.

Kim, K. S. (1994), *'Trade and Industrialization Policies in Korea'* in G. K. Helleiner (ed.), *Trade Policy and Industrialization in Turbulent Times,* New York: Routledge, 317-363.

Kirkpatrick, C. and Weiss, J. (1992), 'Background and Overview' in R. Adhikari, C. Kirkpatrick and Weiss, J. (eds.), *Industrial and Trade Policy Reform in Developing Countries,* Manchester: Manchester University Press, pp 1-9.

Krueger, A.O. (1978), *Foreign Trade Regime and Economic Development: Liberalization Attempts and Consequences*, Cambridge: Ballinger Publishing Company.

Krueger, A.O. (1983), *Trade and Employment in Developing Cou*ntries, NBER, Chicago: Chicago University Press.

Krueger, A.O. and Tuncer, B. (1982), 'Growth of Factor Pr*oductivity in Turkey Manufacturing Industries',* Journal of Development Economics, 11, pp 307-25.

Krugman, P. (1987), 'Is Free Trade Passe?', *Journal of Economic Perspectives*, 1, pp 131-144.

Krugman, P. (1994), *'The Myth of Asian Miracle'*, Foreign Affairs, 73 (6), pp 62-75.

Kwon, J. K. (1986), 'Capital Utilization, Economies of Scale and Technical Change in the Growth of Total Factor Productivity', *Journal of Development Economics,* 24, pp 75-89.

Kyrgyz Republic Official Website, http://stat-gvc.*bishkek.su*

Lewis, W. A. (1955), *The Theory of Economic Growth*, London: Allen and Unwin.

Little, I.M.D., Scitovsky, T. and Scott, M. (1970*), Industry and Trade in Some Developing Countries: A Comparative Study,* New York: Oxford University Press.

Mahfuzur Rahman, A.H.M. (1973), *Exports of Manufactures from Developing Countries- A Study in Comparative Advantage*, Rotterdam.

Michalopoulos, C. (1998), *'WTO Accession for Countries in Transition'*, Downloaded from the web:
http:\\bank.org/html/Publications/Workingpapers/wps1900series/wps1934/wps193

Molnar, E. and Ojala, L. (2003), *'Transport and Trade facilitation Issues in the CIS-7, Kazakhstan and Turkmenistan'*, paper prepared for the Lucerne Conference of the CIS-7 Initiative, 20th-22 January 2003 (downloaded from the web).

Morrison, T.K. (1976a), *Manufactured Exports from Developing Countries*, New York.

Mosley, P. (1993), 'Structural Adjustment: A General Overview, 1980-89' in V.N. Balasubramanyam and Sanjaya Lall (eds.), *Current issues in Development Economics*, London: Macmillan, pp 223-242.

Nishimizu, M. and Page, J. (1990), 'Trade Policy, Market Orientation and Productivity Change in Industry' in J. de Melo, and A, Sapir (eds.), *Trade Theory and Economic Reform: North, South and East: Easy in Honour of Bela Balassa,* Oxford: Basil-Blackwell, pp 246-264.

Nishimuzi, M. and Robinson, S. (1984), 'Trade Policies and *Productivity Change in Semi-industrialized Countries', Journal* of Development Economics, 16, pp 177-210.

Okuda, S. (1994), 'Taiwan's Trade and FDI Policies and Their Effect on Productivity Growth', *The Developing Economies*, XXXII (4), pp 423-434.

Ostery, J.D. (1991), *'Trade Liberalization in Developing Countries Initial Trade Distortion and Imported Intermediate Inputs'*, IMF Staff Papers, 38 (3), pp 447-479.

Pack, H. (1988), 'Industrialization and Trade' in H. Chenery and T.N. Srinivasan (eds.), *Handbook of Development Economics'*, Vol. I, Amsterdam: North-Holland, pp 334-380.

Pack, H. (1984a), 'Total factor Productivity and Its Determinants: Some International Comparisons' in G. Ranis, R. L. West, M. W. Leiserson and S. T. Morris (eds.), *Comparative Development Prospective: Essay in Honor of Lloyd George Reynolds.* Boulder, Colorado: Westview Press, pp 17-41.

Papageorgiou, D., Choski, A. and Michaely, M. (1991), *Liberalizing Foreign Trade in Developing Countries: The Lessons of Experience*, Vols 5 and 7, Oxford: Basil Blackwell.

Perkins, F., Yuxin, Z. and Young, C. (1993), 'The Impact of Reform on Productivity Growth in Chinese Industry: A Case of Xiamen Special Economic Zone', *Asian Economic Journal*, 7 (2), pp 107-146.

Pomfret, Ricard. (2005), Global Integration, Growth and Equity in Kazakhstan', in Sharma and Morrissey (eds.), *Trade, growth and Inequality in developing countries,* Routledge: London.

Pomfret, Richard (1995), *The Economies of Central Asia*, Princeton University Press: Princeton, NJ.

Prim, P. (1992), 'Industry's Response to Market Liberalization in China: Evidence from Jiangsu Province', *Economic Development and Cultural Change*, 41 (1), pp 27-50.

Regmi, G. P. (1994), *Industrial Growth in Nepal: A Sectoral and Regional Analysis,* New Delhi: Oxford and IBM Publishing Co. Pvt. Ltd.

Republic of Tajikistan Official Website, http://www.privatization.tajikistan.com

Rodrik, D. (1992a), 'The Limits of Trade Policy Reform in Developing Countries', *Journal of Economic Perspectives*, 6, (1), pp 87-105.

Rodrik, D. (1992b), 'Closing the Technology Gap: Does Trade Liberalization Really Help?', in G.K. Helleiner (ed.), *Trade Policy, Industrialization and Development: New Perspectives* , Oxford: Claredon Press, pp 155-175.

Rodrik, D. (1992c), *'Conceptual Issues in the Design of Trade Policy for Industrialization'*, World Development, 20 (3), pp 309-319.

Romer, P. (1986), 'Increasing Returns and Long-run Growth'*, Journal of Political Economy,* 94 (5), pp 1002-1037.

Sharma, K. (1999), *Trade Liberalization and Manufacturing Performance in Developing Countries: New Evidence from Nepal*, Nova Science: New York.

Sharma, K. and Morrissey, O. (2005), *Trade Growth and Inequality in the Era of Globalization,* London, Routledge.

Siegelbaum, P. L. et al. (2002), *'Structural Adjustment in the Transition: Case Studies from Albania, Azerbaijan, Kyrgyz Republic and Moldova'*, World Bank Discussion Paper No. 429.

Stein, H. (1992), *'Deindustrialization, Adjustment, the World Bank and the IMF in Africa'*, World Development, 20 (1), pp 83-95.

Thomas, V. (1989), *'Developing Country Experience in Trade Reform', Working Paper Series,* World Bank, Washington.

Tsao, Y. (1985), 'Growth without Productivity: Singapore Manufacturing in the 1970s', *Journal of Development Economics*, 18, pp 25-38.

Tybout J., de Melo, J. and Corbo, V. (1991), 'The Effects of Trade Reforms Scale and Technical Efficiency: New Evidence From Chile', *Journal of International Economics,* 31, pp 4-50.

UNCTAD, (2002), *Trade* and Development Report (2002) Part II, UN: NY and Geneva .

UNCTAD, (1969), *Study on World Demand for and Supply of Manufactures and Semi-manufactures of Export Interest to the Developing Countries*, TD/B/C.2/91, Geneva.

UNESCAP, (2004), '*Economic and social survey of Asia and the Pacific 2004'*, ESCAP, Bangkok

UNIDO, (1974), *Industrial Development Survey - Special Issue for the Second General Conference of UNIDO*, New York: United Nations.

Urata, S. and Yokota, K. (1994), 'Trade Liberalization and Productivity Growth in Thailand', *The Developing Economies*, XXXII (4), pp 444-459.

Verdoorn, P.J. (1949), 'Fattori Che Regolano lo Suiluppo della Productivita del Lavoro', *L' industria*, pp 3-11.

World Bank, (1987), *World Development Report*, London: Oxford University Press.

World Bank, (1993), *The East Asian Miracle*, London: Oxford University Press.

World Bank, (2001), *World Development Report* 2000/2001, World Bank: Washington DC.

World Bank, (2002), *World Development Report* 2001/2002, World Bank: Washington. DC.

World Bank, (2004), *World Development Indicator database*, August 2004.

World Bank, (2004), *World Development Report, Making Services Work for Poor People.* USA: Oxford University Press.

World Bank Website, Doingbusiness, downloaded on 2 April 2005

WTO. (1994), *'Results of the Uruguay Round'*, WTO: Geneva

Young, A. (1995), 'The Tyranny of Numbers: Confronting the Statistical Realities of the East Asian Growth Experience', *Quarterly Journal of Economics*, pp 641-680

INDEX

A

access, 4, 23, 27, 38, 57, 58, 63, 85, 86, 90, 91, 92
accountability, 16, 21
accounting, 75
accumulation, 35, 36, 41
advertising, 90
Afghanistan, 4, 16, 53, 57
Africa, 6, 10, 67, 73, 74
age, 6, 104, 110
aggregates, 10
agricultural exports, 66, 80
agriculture, 5, 12, 60, 66, 70, 97, 98, 101, 105, 111
Albania, 132
alcohol, 55
alternatives, 92
aluminium, 5, 20, 56, 60, 70, 79, 84, 89, 97
annual rate, 36
Argentina, 32
Armenia, 46, 54
Asia, 4, 15, 47, 67, 73, 74, 76, 127, 132
Asian countries, 2, 4, 5, 12, 21, 33, 62, 75, 76, 84, 100
assessment, 45, 65
association, 37, 38, 42
ATP, 124
attention, 8, 23
Australia, viii, 53, 67, 73, 74
Austria, 57
authority, 67, 96
autonomy, 47
availability, 27, 30, 31, 37
average variable cost, 29
Azerbaijan, 46, 54, 82, 132

B

baggage, 115, 116
banking, 43, 47, 48, 49, 58, 59, 60, 92
banks, 27, 47, 49, 57, 58, 59, 92
barriers, 1, 8, 29, 46, 55, 57, 99
barriers to entry, 29
base year, 11, 66, 75
basic services, 8, 92
Belarus, v, 46, 54, 57, 117, 121
beverages, 119
Bhagwati, 24, 27, 29, 30, 32, 128
Bhutan, 21
bias, 30
black market, 24, 25
blocks, 20
bonds, 91
borrowers, 92
Brazil, 32, 34, 38
budget deficit, 12
Bulgaria, 57
business environment, 87, 88, 89, 94, 97

C

Canada, 53
capital flows, 125
capital goods, 24, 27
capital input, 40
capital intensive, 37, 42, 62
capital output ratio, 32
capital-labour ratio, 42
case study, 36
Caspian Sea, 4
Caucasus, v, 117
Central Asia, v, vi, vii, 1, 2, 3, 4, 5, 6, 7, 8, 9, 10, 11, 12, 21, 46, 57, 62, 67, 74, 75, 76, 80, 84, 85, 86, 87, 94, 95, 98, 99, 100, 117, 121, 125, 129, 131
central bank, 49
certificate, 91
channels, 2
children, viii, 6, 103, 109
Chile, 41
China, 4, 12, 16, 39, 53, 57, 80, 121, 132
civil war, 16, 93
closed economy, 98
closure, 38
CO2, 104, 110
coal, 18, 66, 70, 72
collateral, 58, 88, 92
Colombia, 32
commercial bank, 47, 56, 57, 58, 92
commodity, 25, 26, 32, 75, 84, 90
commodity markets, 32
common external tariff, 57
Commonwealth of Independent States, 21
communication, 7, 13, 16, 52
community, 55, 58, 63, 92, 97
comparative advantage, vii, 2, 8, 25, 30, 42, 83, 86, 90, 95, 96
competition, 23, 24, 27, 33, 34, 40, 55, 97
competition policy, 97
competitiveness, 97
components, 38
composition, 66, 67
concentration, 36
constant prices, 15
construction, 34
consumers, 24
consumption, 2, 8, 11, 23, 31, 89, 93, 96
context, 4, 20, 62, 83, 95, 96, 98, 100
control, 8, 12, 43, 60, 83, 97, 98, 100, 101, 123
copper, 70
corporations, 60
correlation, 33
corruption, 4, 16, 21, 91
costs, 8, 21, 34, 86, 87, 117
cotton, 18, 20, 59, 60, 70, 79, 84, 89, 97
coverage, 41
covering, 33
credit, 43, 47, 48, 49, 58, 59
crime, 89, 93
crude oil, 72
Cuba, 53
culture, 84, 97, 99
currency, 47, 56, 60, 63
current account, 8, 12, 47, 60, 76, 84
current account deficit, 8, 12, 76, 84
Cyprus, 53
Czech Republic, 57

D

damage, 55, 91
database, 107, 113, 133
debt, 15, 20, 58, 88, 107, 113
debt service, 107, 113
debts, 96
decisions, 8, 90
deficit, 12, 66, 68
delivery, 75, 91, 97
demand, 16, 27, 32, 34, 38, 95
democracy, 4
dependency ratio, 10
dependent variable, 31, 40
deposits, 5
deregulation, 58, 60, 79, 92
devaluation, 36
developed countries, 24, 31, 34
developed nations, 31

developing countries, vii, 1, 2, 4, 21, 22, 26, 27, 30, 31, 33, 34, 35, 119, 131
development assistance, 10, 12, 63, 99
deviation, 16, 21
diffusion, 27
direct investment, 40, 107, 113
distortions, 21, 25, 96
distribution, 52, 60, 62, 80, 96, 97, 119
diversification, 30
diversity, 84, 99
domestic credit, 47
domestic demand, 31, 35
domestic markets, 34
donations, 91
drought, 79
drug trafficking, 20
drugs, 20, 55, 56

E

earnings, 20, 60, 66, 79, 84, 97
East Asia, 1, 2, 6, 10, 127, 133
Eastern Europe, 2
economic development, 31
economic growth, 2, 27
economic indicator, 13, 15, 20
economic policy, 43
economics, 1, 27
economies of scale, 27, 29, 30, 33, 34, 36, 38
Egypt, 37
electricity, 5, 7, 8, 15, 20, 41, 60, 62, 67, 70, 72, 75, 79, 80, 83, 84, 96, 97, 98, 101
employees, 24, 37, 48
employment, 1, 5, 16, 20, 21, 29, 30, 32, 45, 75, 83, 95, 97, 98, 100, 101
employment growth, 1, 83, 98, 101
energy, 13, 16, 49, 52, 67, 70, 97
enrollment, 104, 110
entrepreneurs, 16, 24, 36, 87
environment, 25, 35, 37, 39, 40, 45, 63, 83, 87, 90, 91, 99, 100, 124
environmental regulations, 117
equipment, 27, 29, 39, 40, 70, 119
estimation problems, 43
Estonia, 46
EU, 76
Eurasia, 46, 121
Europe, 6, 10, 56, 67, 73, 74
evidence, 37, 55
exchange rate, 24, 47, 60, 63, 117
exercise, 4
export promotion, 29, 31, 43
export subsidies, 25
exports, 1, 2, 20, 24, 25, 27, 29, 30, 31, 32, 33, 38, 42, 43, 45, 55, 56, 57, 60, 62, 65, 66, 67, 68, 70, 75, 76, 79, 81, 83, 85, 86, 87, 90, 92, 96, 97, 98, 99, 107, 113, 119, 125
exposure, 2, 27, 96
external shocks, 20, 32, 35, 79

F

failure, 115
farmers, 58
farms, 48
fertilizers, 56, 72
finance, 12, 13, 58, 92
financial institutions, 49, 59, 63
financial resources, 2
financing, 24, 59, 117
firms, 2, 24, 27, 37, 38, 39, 42, 48, 61, 96
fluctuations, 75, 83, 96
food, 8
foreign aid, 12, 30
foreign banks, 47, 58
foreign direct investment, 40, 48, 87, 125
foreign exchange, 2, 24, 27, 30, 47, 60, 96
foreign firms, 27, 39
foreign investment, 2, 21, 30, 36, 38, 48, 62, 80, 83, 96, 97, 100
free trade, 33, 57, 83, 98, 101
free trade area, 33, 98, 101
freedom, 115
fruits, 69, 70, 80, 90, 97
full capacity, 24

G

GATT, v, 56, 115
GDP, 5, 7, 8, 9, 12, 13, 14, 15, 16, 17, 18, 20, 30, 31, 32, 33, 35, 38, 47, 49, 50, 58, 59, 60, 61, 65, 66, 68, 76, 80, 83, 84, 87, 93, 96, 105, 106, 111, 112, 125
GDP per capita, 31
generation, 15, 62, 67, 79, 80, 97
Georgia, 46, 54, 57
Germany, 53
global economy, 1
global trade, 124
globalization, 2, 4
goals, 24
gold, 5, 75, 86, 97
goods and services, 10, 15, 17, 95, 105, 106, 107, 111, 112, 113
governance, 4, 8, 15, 20, 85, 87, 88, 99
government, 10, 24, 26, 36, 47, 55, 56, 58, 60, 91, 93, 96, 117, 128
government expenditure, 10
government intervention, 58
graduate students, vii
grants, 106, 112
Great Britain, 53
groups, 120
growth, vii, 1, 2, 8, 12, 23, 24, 27, 29, 30, 32, 33, 34, 35, 36, 37, 38, 39, 40, 41, 42, 43, 45, 65, 79, 84, 88, 92, 93, 94, 95, 96, 98, 99, 101, 103, 105, 109, 111, 119, 125, 131
growth rate, 39, 41, 95

H

harm, 28
harmonization, 56, 84, 95, 99
health, 93, 104, 109
heavy oil, 72
heteroscedasticity, 43
hip, 35, 41
HIV, 104, 110
Hong Kong, vii, 35
human development, 88, 89
human development index, 89
human rights, 4
hunting, 52
hypothesis, 29, 38, 41

I

ideas, 27
imbalances, vii, 1
IMF, 35, 42, 46, 55, 59, 61, 63, 89, 93, 121, 128, 129, 131, 132
immunization, 6, 104, 110
implementation, 60, 94, 97
import penetration, 35, 40
import substitution, 32, 34, 38, 41
imports, 10, 20, 25, 26, 27, 37, 38, 55, 56, 57, 63, 65, 66, 67, 75, 76, 79, 80, 82, 83, 86, 90, 96, 97
in transition, 94, 129
incentive effect, 26
incentives, 28, 48, 62, 100
income, 2, 5, 6, 10, 11, 12, 20, 24, 32, 33, 48, 87, 88, 89, 93, 96, 125
income distribution, 32
income inequality, 33
income tax, 48
independence, vii, 2, 5, 20, 57, 83, 85, 93
independent variable, 30, 40, 41, 42
India, 24, 33, 53, 56, 57, 128
indicators, 5, 13, 15, 20, 50
indices, 40, 41, 43, 68
indigenous, 36
Indonesia, 53
industry, 13, 32, 34, 37, 39, 42, 43, 52, 79, 105, 111
inefficiency, 26, 58, 67, 75, 84, 97
inequality, 12, 88, 89, 93
inflation, 8, 12, 31, 87
influence, 31
infrastructure, 2, 4, 5, 8, 12, 15, 16, 20, 29, 42, 57, 62, 75, 80, 88, 90, 93, 94, 98, 100, 106, 112
innovation, 27, 36
input, 21, 31, 34, 40, 41, 60, 79
inspections, 91

instability, 117
institutions, 1, 2, 4, 5, 8, 12, 15, 20, 29, 62, 63, 75, 87, 88, 93, 94, 99, 100
instruments, 119
integration, vii, 1, 2, 4, 20, 21, 45, 62, 80, 85, 87, 91, 96, 98, 99, 100, 129
intellectual property, 62
intensity, 31, 39, 40, 42
interdependence, 1
interest, 35, 48, 58, 87, 92
interest rates, 48, 58, 87, 92
International Monetary Fund, 46
international trade, 1, 32, 46, 55, 83, 85, 90, 92, 98, 101
intra-regional trade, 8
investment, 1, 2, 4, 8, 15, 16, 33, 35, 42, 45, 48, 55, 62, 83, 86, 88, 92, 93, 95, 96, 98, 100, 101
investors, 48, 62, 87
Iran, 4, 57, 81, 82, 121
Ireland, 53
iron, 39
Israel, 53
Italy, 53, 81

J

Japan, 32, 34, 39, 54
jobs, 2, 96, 100
justification, 31

K

Kazakhstan, 2, 4, 5, 6, 7, 9, 10, 11, 12, 46, 54, 56, 57, 67, 73, 74, 75, 76, 81, 82, 86, 91, 99, 121, 123, 125, 131
knowledge, 27
Korea, 32, 34, 35, 36, 37, 39, 53, 81
Kuwait, 57
Kyrgyzstan, v, 4, 5, 11, 13, 14, 15, 16, 20, 21, 22, 23, 46, 47, 48, 49, 50, 57, 63, 66, 75, 83, 85, 86, 87, 88, 89, 93, 96, 99, 100, 103

L

labour, 8, 26, 27, 29, 31, 32, 37, 40, 42, 62, 75, 79, 80, 92, 95, 97, 100
labour force, 80
labour market, 29
land, 2, 5, 8, 21, 30, 56, 60, 62, 80, 85, 91, 100
language, 5
Latin America, 6, 10
Latvia, 46
law enforcement, 16
laws, 115
LDCs, 24, 27, 29, 32, 37
lead, 24, 27, 32, 33
learning, 27
lending, 58
liberalization, 12, 28, 29, 32, 36, 38, 39, 41, 42, 43, 63, 99
licenses, 24
links, 34, 86, 90, 92, 99
liquidity, 48, 58
Lithuania, 46, 53
livestock, 12
living standards, 2, 96
loans, 49, 58, 59, 63
location, 2, 21
logistics, 86, 90
long run, 15, 23, 32, 80
lower prices, 48

M

machinery, 39, 119
macroeconomic policies, 43
Malaysia, 34, 53
malnutrition, 104
management, 27, 52, 80, 96
manufactured goods, 31, 57, 62, 67
manufacturing, 7, 20, 27, 29, 30, 32, 33, 34, 35, 36, 37, 38, 39, 40, 41, 42, 43, 48, 51, 62, 66, 70, 98, 101

market, 2, 4, 14, 18, 24, 27, 28, 29, 30, 31, 34, 38, 45, 47, 48, 49, 57, 59, 60, 63, 67, 80, 83, 85, 92, 94, 98, 99, 101
market capitalization, 49, 59
market concentration, 29, 31
market economy, 45, 57, 94, 98
market failure, 29
market share, 28
marketing, 2, 15, 25, 80, 96, 97, 98
markets, 5, 8, 21, 27, 31, 38, 57, 60, 75, 76, 79, 80, 85, 86, 91, 92, 97, 98, 99
measles, 104, 110
measurement, 43
measures, 20, 32, 43, 55, 63, 95, 96
median, 6
membership, 4, 30, 45, 47, 48, 55, 62, 63, 121
metals, 75, 97
methodology, 35, 42, 43
Mexico, 32, 34, 38
Middle East, 6, 10
minimum wage, 29
mining, 7, 13, 98, 101
mobile phone, 90
mobility, 1
mode, 115
model specification, 43
models, 23
Moldova, v, 46, 54, 117
money, 58, 86, 90, 92
Mongolia, 46
monopoly, 24, 60, 80
monopoly profits, 24
mortality, 103, 109
mortality rate, 103, 109
mountains, 16
movement, 27, 99

N

narcotics, 55
national income, 2, 12
natural gas, 8, 72, 79, 97
natural resources, vii, 8, 30, 80, 84, 99
needs, 86
negative relation, 35, 41
Nepal, 21, 56, 132
net exports, 36
Netherlands, 53, 81
network, 4, 8, 79, 80, 97, 101, 123
Norway, 34

O

Oceania, 67, 73, 74
OECD, 87, 88
oil, 5, 35, 71, 79, 104, 110
oils, 71
openness, 31, 33
organizations, 63, 86, 92, 99
orientation, 23, 25, 27, 28, 29, 30, 31, 33, 34, 36, 38, 40, 42, 43
outline, 95
output, 1, 5, 8, 13, 16, 20, 21, 24, 25, 28, 29, 30, 31, 32, 33, 34, 35, 36, 37, 38, 40, 41, 43, 45, 60, 79, 90, 97
ownership, 48, 115
ownership structure, 48

P

Pacific, 6, 7, 10, 127, 132
packaging, 80, 92
Pakistan, 34, 54, 57, 121
per capita income, 2, 4, 5, 11, 20, 89, 93
percentile, 20
permit, 57, 86, 91
perspective, 45
Philippines, 34, 39
Poland, 54
policy reform, 39, 40, 43
political leaders, 24
politics, 1
poor, 6, 8, 12, 15, 20, 32, 36, 38, 42, 57, 62, 75, 80, 85, 87, 88, 89, 90, 91, 94, 95, 96, 97, 100
population, 2, 4, 6, 12, 20, 30, 31, 33, 89, 90, 93, 103
population density, 31
positive relation, 41

positive relationship, 41
potential output, 26
poverty, vii, 1, 2, 12, 15, 20, 58, 88, 89, 93, 94, 95, 96, 100, 103
poverty alleviation, 2, 96, 100
poverty line, 15, 20, 89, 93
power, 4, 38, 79, 80, 119
predictability, 100
pressure, 1, 41
price deflator, 105, 111
prices, 11, 14, 18, 24, 26, 29, 48, 60, 66, 75, 84, 97, 100
principle, 56, 91
private sector, 4, 21, 36, 47, 58, 60, 62, 86, 88, 90, 92, 97, 99, 117, 128
privatization, 12, 16, 29, 43, 47, 48, 50, 60, 61, 90, 95, 96, 97, 99, 101, 132
producers, 5, 92
production, 2, 12, 20, 23, 24, 25, 26, 27, 30, 31, 32, 34, 39, 57, 60, 62, 67, 75, 79, 83, 92, 96, 97, 98
productivity, 13, 23, 24, 27, 28, 29, 33, 34, 35, 36, 37, 38, 39, 40, 41, 42, 43, 45, 48, 91, 98
productivity growth, 23, 24, 27, 28, 29, 33, 34, 36, 37, 38, 39, 40, 42, 43, 98
profits, 24, 25, 62
program, 28, 29, 43, 60
protocol, 123
public enterprises, 12, 42, 47, 95, 101
public investment, 94
public sector, 37, 60
pupil, 6
purchasing power, 11, 83
purchasing power parity, 11

Q

quotas, 24

R

range, 2, 85, 93
ratings, 46, 55
real income, 95
reality, 57
recovery, 88
reflection, 93
reforms, 30, 32, 38, 39, 41, 45, 58, 62
regression, 30, 31, 33, 40
regression analysis, 33
regression equation, 40
regulations, 24, 29, 75, 115, 116, 117
rehabilitation, 57
relationship, 39, 40
religion, 5
remittances, 60
rent, 25, 26, 27, 28, 52, 83, 91, 98, 101
repair, 52
reserves, 5
resource allocation, 2, 30, 33, 96
resources, vii, 5, 24, 25, 26, 30, 35, 63, 80, 83, 84, 97, 98, 99, 101, 104, 110
restructuring, 48
returns, 37
returns to scale, 37
revenue, 12, 47, 60, 61, 91, 95, 106, 112, 117
rewards, 4
Romania, 57
rule of law, 94
rural population, 90
Russia, v, 56, 57, 65, 67, 73, 74, 75, 76, 80, 81, 82, 83, 85, 92, 96, 99, 117, 121

S

sales, 28
sample, 33, 34
secondary data, vii
security, 57, 58, 92
self, 8, 37
semiconductors, 119
service provider, 89
services, 6, 13, 27, 35, 48, 51, 52, 58, 60, 68, 77, 86, 90, 91, 97, 98, 99, 105, 111, 115
severity, 8
shareholders, 58
shares, 11, 33, 58, 67, 73, 74, 79
sheep, 69
shelter, 4, 12

shock, 35
shortage, 24, 30, 47
Siberia, 4
signals, 63, 123
similarity, 84, 99
Singapore, vii, 32, 35, 36, 132
skills, 27
Slovakia, 57
small firms, 61
social activities, 8
social indicator, 4
social security, 51
social services, 52
social welfare, 8
South Asia, 6, 10, 21
South Korea, 35, 129
Soviet Union, vii, 1, 5, 8
Spearman rank correlation coefficient, 32
speed, 45
sports, 51
stability, 12, 16, 21, 80, 98, 100
stages, 47
standards, 4, 63, 96
state control, 97
state-owned banks, 47, 49, 59
state-owned enterprises, 45
statistics, 65
steel, 39
stock, 36, 40, 42, 43
Stolper-Samuelson theorem, 33
strategies, 1, 29, 35, 98
strategy use, 25
substitution, 2, 24, 32, 38, 39, 41, 42, 128
sugar, 67, 70, 72
suppliers, 5, 75
supply, 8, 12, 21, 27, 29, 31, 38, 95, 100
suspects, 36
sustainable growth, 89
Switzerland, 15, 54, 81, 82
systems, 2, 42, 91

T

Taiwan, 32, 33, 35, 38, 40, 128
Tajikistan, v, vii, 2, 4, 5, 6, 7, 8, 9, 10, 11, 12, 16, 17, 18, 20, 21, 22, 23, 45, 46, 48, 54, 55, 56, 57, 58, 59, 60, 61, 62, 63, 65, 73, 74, 75, 76, 77, 79, 80, 81, 83, 85, 87, 89, 90, 92, 93, 95, 96, 97, 98, 99, 100, 109, 121, 123, 125, 132
tariff, 21, 26, 45, 46, 55, 57, 63, 83, 98, 99, 100, 101
teachers, 6
technical change, 37
technical efficiency, 29
technological change, 32
technology, 2, 23, 27, 30, 38, 92, 96, 97, 107, 113
tension, 20, 98, 101
textiles, 62
Thailand, 40
threat, 98, 101
time, vii, 2, 4, 15, 21, 24, 40, 46, 55, 57, 75, 83, 86, 87, 89, 90, 91, 92, 97, 98, 101
TIR, 123
tobacco, 55
total factor productivity, 34
trade, vii, 1, 4, 7, 8, 16, 20, 22, 23, 25, 26, 27, 29, 30, 31, 32, 33, 34, 35, 36, 38, 39, 41, 42, 43, 45, 46, 48, 55, 56, 57, 60, 62, 63, 65, 66, 68, 75, 76, 79, 81, 83, 84, 85, 86, 88, 90, 91, 92, 95, 96, 98, 99, 100, 101, 121, 125
trade agreement, 46, 57
trade deficit, 66, 75
trade diversion, 83, 98, 101
trade liberalization, 31, 32, 41
trade policy, 30, 32, 34, 43, 46, 56
trading, 60, 67, 76, 129
trading partners, 76
traffic, 115, 116, 123
training, 29
training programs, 29
transactions, 47, 55, 58, 60, 65, 83, 85, 89, 90, 92, 98, 101
transition, 5, 8, 37, 57, 94
transition period, 8
transparency, 87, 99, 100

transport, 1, 4, 7, 12, 13, 15, 39, 60, 75, 80, 84, 85, 86, 89, 90, 97, 98, 99, 101, 115, 123
transportation, 8, 16, 21, 60, 86, 87, 90, 115
trend, 8, 12, 39, 40
Turkey, 32, 34, 54, 57, 121, 130
Turkmenistan, 2, 4, 5, 6, 7, 8, 9, 10, 11, 46, 54, 73, 74, 82, 91, 121, 123, 125

U

Ukraine, v, 46, 54, 56, 82, 117
UN, 1, 47, 120, 121, 132
uncertainty, 90, 91
unemployment, vii, 8, 12, 20, 88, 89, 93, 94, 100
unemployment rate, 20
United Kingdom, 81, 82
United Nations, 30, 133
United States, 54, 82
urban areas, 90
Uruguay, 116, 133
Uruguay Round, 116, 133
Uzbekistan, 2, 4, 5, 6, 7, 8, 9, 10, 11, 12, 16, 20, 46, 54, 56, 57, 67, 73, 74, 81, 82, 86, 91, 97, 99, 121, 123, 125

V

values, 6, 14, 18
variable, 30, 37, 39, 43
variables, 31, 35, 38, 39, 41
variation, 34
VAT, 55, 87, 92
vegetable oil, 67, 72
vegetables, 75, 83, 86, 97
vehicles, 52, 83, 98, 101, 123
vessels, 115
Vietnam, 57
violence, 16, 21, 89, 93
voice, 20

W

wages, 88
war, 16, 32
water, 5, 6, 7, 8, 15, 52, 80, 83, 96, 98, 101, 104, 110
water resources, 5, 15, 80, 83, 96
weakness, 100
web, 90, 130, 131
welfare, 8, 23, 26
welfare system, 8
wheat, 60, 67, 72, 79
winter, 16, 90
wool, 70
words, 4
work, 12, 23, 35, 38, 43
workers, 41
World Bank, 1, 6, 10, 16, 20, 21, 33, 35, 39, 43, 68, 88, 89, 90, 93, 125, 128, 129, 132, 133
World Development Report, 6, 133
World Trade Organization, 1, 116
world trading system, 80
WTO, 1, 4, 45, 47, 48, 55, 62, 63, 99, 121, 129, 133

Y

yield, 13
Yugoslavia, 32, 34, 57